The People's SCRUM

Agile Ideas for Revolutionary Transformation

by

Tobias Mayer

Dedicated to Tim Webb and Kert Peterson, two friends and colleagues who informed and inspired my early journey.

Published by Dymaxicon
San Francisco, CA

ISBN 978-1-937965-15-0
www.dymaxicon.com

copy editing by Rayna Mayer
book design by Hillary Louise Johnson
text set in Fontin and Calluna by Jos Buivenga

DYMAXICON

The People's Scrum

Essays 2005-2012

Contents

Culture—The Promised Land

Foreword

by Ron Jeffries

In this foreword, my responsibility is to help you to decide whether to read this book, why read it, and how to read it. The short answers are: "Yes," "Because you'll gain new insights into agile and scrum," and "With a peaceful and open mind." Let me give you a little more on the why and how.

Agile software development and scrum have been around for years. They are quite widespread now, and we are seeing more and more clearly that agile methods are the way to go on a very wide range of projects. Personally, I'd choose to do any project on my plate in agile style—and with over a half-century of software experience, I can say that with some confidence.

Following the widespread acceptance of agile methods, we've seen generally good results. Teams that work this way generally perform better. However, only a few teams seem to get the full benefit that is there for the taking. The reasons vary. Sometimes teams don't use good technical practices. Sometimes they don't make good selections of what to work on. Sometimes they're not managed in a way that works with agile methods.

These "weak" successes seem to me to stem from a common cause: Teams and their management have a shallow understanding of agile ideas, so that when things start to go wrong, they make non-agile decisions. When things go fairly well, as they generally do, they are satisfied, but they do not progress as far as they could. As a team and its management gain a deeper understanding, they are better able to make good choices on how to improve. Their ideals are higher, which keeps them moving forward. They begin to get agile "in their bones," which helps them stay committed and keep moving toward excellence.

Tobias's essays are all aimed at helping you gain that deeper understanding. They ask questions. They offer new ways of looking at things. If you're like me, they may confuse you at first, or even make you angry. This is good.

Tobias has been working in agile software development and scrum for years. As I've observed him, he has often seemed to be looking at things from some odd angle that I couldn't quite figure out. My way of learning is to do things, and to try to understand why they work. I use what I call "mindful practice" to learn new approaches, internalize them, and understand them. And that's how I teach as well. I show people how I do things, I tell them why I do them, and I invite them to try the ideas and pay attention to what happens. I help them to build up their own understanding, and to make their own decisions.

This works for me, in part because I have the habit of thinking as deeply as I can about what's going on, and in part because I have the time to do so. The pressure of day-to-day work makes it hard for many people to stay committed to learning, and so they don't get as far as they might.

Tobias approaches things differently in these essays.

When Tobias and I look at some issue, my immediate reaction is to say, "Do this and see what happens," or to explain what is going on in terms of the forces that are at play in the situation. Tobias sees the same concern, and somehow turns it inside out. I can tell we're thinking about the same problem, but his view on it is so different from mine that it often stops me short. This used to make me angry sometimes, because he seemed not to be getting it at all. Finally, I realized that it was usually me who wasn't getting it. This means we need to approach what he writes in a way that will let his ideas into our heads.

There are some books and websites that I read for immediate

information or ideas about something to do right now. For me, this book needs to be read quietly and in peace. I need to let it soak in gently. When I feel like shouting "Tobias, NOOOO!" it means that Tobias has ahold of another part of the issue than I'm looking at. I need to calm down and try to figure out why he'd say that, what he's seeing that I'm not seeing.

I don't always agree with what Tobias says, though in the end I often do. I do always gain an insight into the topic of the essay. I gain a broader understanding of the people who make up our projects. Since agile is about "Individuals and Interactions," that's a good thing.

Welcome to Tobias's book. I like it, and I think you will like it as well.

Author's Introduction

I came to software development late in life—I was in my mid-thirties before I used a computer in any capacity, and then only because I had to. I had started a job as a life skills trainer for teenagers on probation, and was required to develop curriculums, track progress and submit reports. Spreadsheet and word processing skills were a requirement. Computers were not something that interested me, in fact they scared me; I didn't see their value, and I did my best to avoid any contact. But necessity compels, and once I learned the basics I was immediately intrigued, and wanted to delve below the surface, get my hands dirty with ones and zeros and machine instructions, see how this thing worked, and what I could do to change it. I have a tinkerer's soul.

I wrote my first programs in DOS QBasic, and even with such a coarse language I discovered, contrary to my expectations, that only a small part of computer programming was concerned with math and logic—the rest was pure poetry. I was hooked. A year later I enrolled in a BSc program at London South Bank University, graduating in 1999 and launching into a new career.

My background before this had been in construction, graphic design, technical theatre, and later as a trainer and facilitator with social services and the probation system, working in creative ways with various disempowered groups and individuals towards personal self-actualization. This later work was the furthest thing imaginable from software development, and yet it is the experience that has served me best in the world of agile coaching and consulting. Disenfranchised teenagers struggling in inner cities and software engineers working in large, oppressive corporations—there are more similarities than differences. Both groups are silenced; both have much to say. The agile consultant's skill lies in giving voice to the silent majority, in freeing the creative, sometimes rebellious spirit, and then getting out of the way.

In my third year of study I had the opportunity to spend a year in research before completing my degree. I sensed very early on that using a defined process to manage a creative endeavor was a non-starter, and could only cause pain. My natural inclination was to make things up as I went along. My research was thus focused on software process, specifically looking for what had been gained and what had been lost as the software world moved from an anarchic, hacking culture to a corporate, controlled one. It didn't take me long to discover Kent Beck's early work on extreme programming (XP), in which I recognized a return to the human values so present in the original hackers of the '60s and '70s—yet with added discipline. I was intrigued. It would be a few years before I could put this theory into practice, but the seed of agility was sown. Beck's work—so lightweight and people-centric—was controversial and shocking to academics and practitioners alike, many of whom still clung to the idea that more process, not less, was needed to control outcomes. I found myself defending an idea I knew little about against seasoned veterans of the industry, simply because I intuitively felt Beck had it right, and the rest of the industry were getting it more and more wrong.

Discovering Agile

My graduation in 1999 coincided with my family's move from London to Palo Alto. It was pure coincidence that my (then) wife's family home was in the heart of the computer industry. We moved here for family reasons, not work ones, yet I quickly found a job with a small startup building website testing tools.

Testing and measuring had both been areas of interest for me during my study years, so this was a good fit.

Coming to software development at the turn of the century, I was spared a lot of the nonsense most developers of my generation had to work through in the '80s and '90s—the wearing of suits to work, the defined, top-down processes, the idea that programmers were cogs in a big wheel of business, disposable and replaceable with mechanistic code generators or cheap, third world labor. Agile was already beginning to stir as a movement—the first scrum patterns paper was written in 1993, and Tom Gilb's evolutionary project management (Evo), although little-practiced, was an idea that had been around for over ten years already. The "scientific management" models our industry had inexplicably adopted from the 19th century industrial efficiency work of Frederick W. Taylor were far from gone, but they were surely being eroded as the internet world challenged us to move at increased speed.

Silicon Valley was going crazy in the late '90s: startups were being born daily and dying just as quickly, and people were becoming overnight millionaires, only to lose it all a few months later. The company I worked for was a chaotic, micro-management circus. I struggled to implement some good development and testing practices, but the drive to keep the customer happy overrode any concerns about quality, sustainability and worker health. The irony is that we were writing tools to help others improve quality. But who tests the testing tools?

I did learn a lot about testing during that time, and because of the nature of our business I attended and spoke at the Quality Week conferences in Europe and the USA. I met Lisa Crispin and Tip House at one of these, and they introduced me to the idea of "extreme testing." The concept intrigued and excited me, reviving my interest in extreme programming and prompting me to return to Kent Beck's work. I bought his recent book, but sadly, it sat on my shelf at work for the next year, collecting dust—in my few spare moments I preferred sleep to reading.

The company I worked for ran out of money at the end of 2001, stopped paying salaries and then finally collapsed in 2002; I found myself temporarily out of work—and broke. After working in the construction industry again for a few months, I was eventually offered a temporary position at Yahoo! which later turned into a full time role.

Still intrigued by the XP approach, I made time to return to Beck's book, and we explored the ideas within our group. We cannot claim to have been an XP team, but we were able to practice pair-programming, regular refactoring, continuous integration, and unit testing. I joined the agile-testing online discussion group started in 2000 by Lisa Crispin and Brian Marick and learned better ways to test software, earlier in the process. We removed the developer/QA barrier and began working as a single team, even having developer/tester pairing for large chunks of the day. It was something. It was meaningful. We enjoyed our work, and yet we knew we had a long way to go.

An opportunity to socialize this learning more widely came in 2003, when I was promoted into a management position, leading a development team of twelve. My own manager allowed me the freedom to dive further into the agile space and very soon I discovered scrum. With its lightweight, team-centric approach scrum offered a refreshing opportunity to manage work in a way that felt more natural and intuitive. The scrum concept of self-organizing teams closely paralleled the work I had done in the youth and community field.

In early 2004 I read the two scrum books available at the time and participated in Ken Schwaber and Kert Peterson's Certified ScrumMaster training. For the next six months our team practiced stealth-scrum, keeping detailed metrics of defect counts, throughput time, deadlines, downtime, and other measures of interest, comparing the numbers with previous projects we'd worked on. We could honestly show a 500+% improvement in quality and time-to-market. It was remarkable.

In January 2005, following visits and talks from well-known agilists Ken Schwaber, Jeff Sutherland and Mike Cohn, the product organization at Yahoo! decided to undertake a scrum pilot project with five groups. I changed roles at that point, and became part of the newly formed agile process team—a team of three responsible for implementing the pilot project and coaching the teams. As is commonly the case with these kinds of grassroots experiments within large organizations, our successes were modest, but the seeds of change had been sown, and continue to flourish today.

The Scrum Years

I left Yahoo! In August 2005 to pursue a career as an independent scrum trainer and coach. I had taught a couple of CSM classes with Ken Schwaber and achieved the status of Certified Scrum Trainer (CST) with the newly formed Scrum Alliance. In 2005 there were about 20 CSTs worldwide, so opportunities were great. I believed in scrum as a way of working, but I always struggled with the idea of certification. It seemed to hark back to exactly what we wanted to escape from: a hierarchical, checkbox model of management.

This disconnect caused problems with my scrum career right from the start, as clearly indicated by my checkered history with the Scrum Alliance—scrum's main controlling body. I was decertified as a trainer in 2007, due to my unwillingness to agree to policy decisions. I was reinstated in 2008, at Ken Schwaber's invitation, but then had to go through a whole new application process. I continued to battle against SA policy and the growing bureaucracy around certification programs, then surprisingly, following Schwaber's dismissal as chairman of the board at the end of 2009, I was offered the role of creative director by the new chairman. I accepted in the hope of changing the organization from within. I lasted eight months in this role, finally quitting in August 2010, when I also surrendered all my Scrum Alliance certifications. I couldn't, with any integrity, continue to hold and offer certifications that I fundamentally felt represented a flawed and hypocritical system. I wrote a public disclosure of my decision at the time, drawing a huge barrage of comments, at both extremes of opinion.

My entanglements with the Scrum Alliance aside, I spent the years 2005 to 2012 working as a consultant, coach, trainer and facilitator with many organizations, both large and small, that were attempting to introduce more lightweight, agile methods into their organizations and had sought me out as some kind of expert. I learned a lot on this journey, and began writing about my ideas and experiences in late 2005 on the blogs Agile Thinking and later (as I grew bolder), Agile Anarchy. The essays offered here grew out of my writing during that seven-year period.

Coming full circle, I welcomed the opportunity to rejoin Yahoo! in January 2013, as I was putting the finishing touches to this book. I can see the growth of understanding and appreciation for agile that has developed over the past eight years. There is still far to go—here and in business in general—to truly embrace the cultural transformation necessary to accommodate this way of working and ensure its stickiness once the consultants and coaches go away, but it is exciting to participate in a meaningful journey of transformation.

The Essays

Blog writing is a just-in-time process, where ideas can be aired to see how they feel. As E.M. Forster said, "How do I know what I think until I see what I say?" Sometimes the ideas I threw out felt good, sometimes they made me uncomfortable, and other times they just seemed ridiculous. The process of writing and sharing allowed me to become more discerning, to develop clarity about what I was doing and what I believed in. The essays offered in this book are personal favorites selected from a body of work written between 2005 and 2012: ideas and practices I can still stand behind today. In some instances the ideas are substantially reworked from the original, and in others, surprisingly not at all.

Some of the essays are rooted in pragmatism, others in idealism, some in experience, others in abstract thought. They do not need to be read in the order they are presented, but can be read as need or desire suggests. They do presuppose a basic familiarity with scrum and other agile concepts, so if you are someone with little or no knowledge of scrum, please begin by reading Appendix 1: Scrum—A Simple Framework for Complex Problems.

It is my fond hope that after spending some time with this book you, the reader, will experience an aha moment or two, and perhaps be inspired to explore some of the ideas and practices in your own work environments. At the very least, I hope you find ideas to inspire disagreement, and perhaps help to clarify your own thinking, however different it may be to what is offered here.

Tobias Mayer, Palo Alto, February 2013

People

The Intrepid Explorers

I am interested in people and how they interact. I like people, probably more than any other single thing in the world. I am intrigued by the ways we live, what we think, the things we do, the choices we make... intrigued and baffled.

People are puzzles waiting to be solved, but mostly unsolvable. We selectively and cautiously share our stories, observing social mores and cultural etiquette; we distribute ourselves and hide behind masks.

It is hard to gather all the pieces back into one place, to peel away the facades and see the core beauty of another. Though difficult, it should always be a quest.

A New Way of Thinking

I'd like to offer you a vision. Imagine your days at work being filled with laughter and passion, you and your co-workers imbued with a feeling of camaraderie, dwelling in a climate of excitement, purpose and hope, spending your time in an environment that fosters listening, open communication and fast collaboration. Imagine a workspace that harks back to playgrounds of childhood where invention and innovation were a natural part of every interaction. Imagine being responsible for your own physical space, your own workload, your own pace. Imagine delivering high-quality work, frequently, to delighted, relaxed customers.

You can turn that imagination into reality, using a simple and well-understood mechanism for getting from wherever you are now to where you would like to be. And no, despite the title of this book, that mechanism is not scrum. No framework, process or methodology alone can realize this vision. Nor is it leadership, in any of its many guises, although many of us would love to turn to our leaders for guidance on this—or find new leaders when ours fail to deliver. No. There is only one thing that can bring this vision to life. It is you.

More specifically, it is the interaction of your moving parts: body, mind, heart, spirit, and your personal relationship to those you work with. Successful product development comes from happy, impassioned individuals and highly motivated, energized teams.

So how does scrum help?

Scrum will offer you structure and boundaries to contain

and guide your creativity. A common misconception holds that scrum is a methodology similar to lean, six sigma, rapid application development, unified process, or even kanban. Scrum is certainly taught from that perspective, but to think of it like this is to miss its essence. Scrum is best understood as a scaffold—a framework for building new products, or for guiding complex projects; it is not a formula for success, and it most certainly isn't the next "silver bullet." Scrum represents a movement away from hierarchical, command-and-control systems towards trust and self-organization.

Scrum is rooted in the principles of complex adaptive systems, the branch of systems science that deals with chaotic phenomena like economies and ecosystems where patterns of organization emerge from within, rather than being imposed from the outside. Embracing this chaos, scrum seeks to manage complex problems through frequent inspection, self-organization and just-in-time decision making.

Scrum consists of a few core rules and practices (outlined in Appendix I) which, although very simple, are utterly essential. Each rule and practice is part of a synergistic whole, and to drop one part is to destroy that synergy. Half measures avail nothing—they won't even avail half. When you adhere to the guidelines of scrum, and understand the underlying principles, a process will emerge that is suited to your own context.

According to co-founder Ken Schwaber, scrum makes one promise only: It will help you fail in thirty days or less. That's it. Organizational dysfunction will begin to surface as the work plays out. Healing from that dysfunction is up to you. What scrum can give you is a space to be human, to try, to fail, to reflect and to try again. Putting the simple scrum framework in place at your organization will be the first step towards fostering an environment of safety and trust; in time this will lead to the release of human potential, guiding you towards innovation and success.

Scrum itself does not prescribe or promise any of this. It is simply a structure which will allow those things to emerge, rather like a bamboo frame allows a tomato plant to bear fruit. It is the people—you and your teammates and your managers—who will make the changes that lead to new behaviors and new ways of thinking. An organization seriously investing in scrum will find its own way of working within the simple framework. The people doing the work will discover the appropriate set of practices best suited to optimize their organization's return on investment. People will create a happier work environment, not process.

Remember, scrum is not a rigid methodology; it continues to evolve, to adapt. Similar to a strategy game, such as chess, you begin with a few clear and simple rules. Once those rules or guidelines are understood and practiced a multitude of strategies, i.e. scrum implementations are possible. Most importantly, scrum is context-dependent; the needs of the organization should drive the implementation. There is no formula, no prescription, no defined set of steps. Scrum does not tell you how to do scrum.

March 22, 2008

The Heart of Scrum

The longer I teach and coach scrum, the more I become convinced that the physical workflow board is the heart of scrum. Without the workflow board, a team has no center, no focus, no hub. The workflow board, when truly understood, becomes the spiritual home of the team, its church if you like. Team members gather around the board to argue, discuss and innovate, to align themselves with each other, to course-correct, to learn, to celebrate.

The workflow board (aka taskboard), with its index cards, sticky notes, tape, flags and stickers, generates collaboration. It is visual, it is tactile, it is larger than life (it is much, much larger than a computer screen). It stands as a big, visible marker of our progress and of our character. It proclaims who we are as a team. It is our identity. The workflow board tells the truth, and it spreads the message: we are unafraid.

The workflow board is often described as the water cooler of the new paradigm. This parallel, while well-meaning, is actually doing the workflow board a disservice. Yes, it is a place to gather, to talk. No, it is not a place to complain, to gossip, to blow off steam. The workflow board is a place to regenerate oneself, to reconnect, to draw breath. It represents a running toward, not a running away from.

Scrum is the antithesis of the corporate cubicle divide-and-conquer mentality. We don't need table tennis and foosball to appease us, to create an artificial work-life balance. We don't need fun as an afterthought to work. Work is fun. We don't require water cooler moments and cigarette breaks in order to exercise our deep, human need for conversation, for interaction. In scrum we live this way. All day, every day.

Scrum is about whole people, not about skills. Scrum is not I, but We. It is about sharing, learning, continuous improvement, vibrant interaction, passionate collaboration, and personal growth. Scrum is about tribes, it is about building community. Each tribal member needs a sense of belonging, a personal quest. Whole tribes need gathering places, they need sacred objects, they need focus and they need pulse. Scrum supports this way of being. The workflow board and its emergent environment provide the central life-force from which these things are born.

To live, to truly live, scrum needs a heart. That heart is the workflow board. Without it scrum looks and feels insipid. It is weak, and thin. It loses its focus, and without an outside controller (e.g. coach, champion) to continually pump life into it, the effort will soon dissolve back into the dysfunctional process it was brought in to replace. Without its heart, scrum has no power.

One of the kindest services a scrum master can do for his or her team and for the organization as a whole is to create transparency—to radiate information. Transparency allows us to see flaws, and when we see the flaws we can make the choice to do something about them. We can stop being victims of process and start being warriors of change.

If teams truly begin to own their workflow boards, and discover how to use them to live the principle of transparency, this humble sticky note tool will rise above being just a utilitarian artifact. Each team can take their workflow board from a useful tool to an object of beauty and inspiration. And the way I see it, that is the workflow board's rightful place. The heart thrives on love.

August 3rd, 2009

Self-Organization and Anarchy

Self-organization is often equated with anarchy, causing management to shy away from the concept for fear of losing control. Jim Highsmith, a well-known agilist, has endorsed that mindset, challenging the concept of self-organization and indicating it is not only unnecessary, but actually detrimental to agile adoption.[1] This is tragic. Agile practice without self-organization is just another management-led process, and will stay rooted in the existing status quo.

Perhaps self-organization is chaotic, even anarchic. Let's embrace that. Anarchism need not be thought of as a negative force, especially when understood by the definition offered by the American Heritage College Dictionary: "Rejection of all forms of coercive control and authority," and by other non-inflammatory sources like L. Susan Brown, who helps clarify the true meaning of the idea: "While the popular understanding of anarchism is of a violent, anti-State movement, anarchism is a much more subtle and nuanced tradition than a simple opposition to government power. Anarchists oppose the idea that power and domination are necessary for society, and instead advocate more co-operative, anti-hierarchical forms of social, political and economic organization."

I am an anarchist at heart, and I believe in grassroots revolution as a way to fundamentally change the way we think about building software. I believe this because, without a doubt,

[1] Jim Highsmith, "No More Self-Organizing Teams," *The Cutter Blog*, September 13, 2007

the people writing the software are, unsurprisingly, those who know best how to write the software. Unless they self-organize to solve the immensely complex problems software presents, the results are likely to be thin on innovation, with customers only ever getting what they think they want, rather than what they actually need. I use my anarchistic tendency to encourage people to challenge blind authority and reconceive ideas; it is a powerful and energizing approach.

Anarchism has played a useful role in the history of democracy. I think it also has a useful role to play in the agile space. Let's not discard it so quickly. Jesus of Nazareth was an anarchist, so was Gandhi. Both confronted the status quo, and both initiated great change. In agile we are also seeking great change. What can we learn?

The danger that arises when established agilists decry self-organization is that those clinging on to the traditional corporate mindset will jump on the bandwagon to utterly dismiss the idea and fall back into old command-and-control habits, believing they were right all along. Claiming self-organization has no place in the new paradigm is dismissive of the great number of good people who are creating magic in staid, crippled, half-dead corporations by injecting the passion of engagement and autonomy. Self-organization may well be misunderstood—and I agree that it often is—but that is not cause to dismiss it out of hand. Seek to enlighten rather than to appease.

Self-organization is a key principle of scrum. The concept is utterly essential to changing the way people in the software industry think about their value system, and about how they work together across organizational tiers.

Good self-organization does not exclude leadership. The need for a leader, and more importantly the right type of leader, will emerge from the wisdom of the team, and should never be imposed ahead of time, or indeed at any time. People outside of the team are not the best positioned to know what the team requires. Well-functioning, self-organized teams will request leaders as needed. I have seen this, and it is good.

September 13th, 2007

Shock Therapy... or Compassion?

Jeff Sutherland and Scott Downey, working together at MySpace, have created something they are calling "shock therapy for scrum,"[1] which they claim bootstraps teams to become "hyper-productive."

While there is much of value in their case study, something about the approach disturbs me. The writers use terms like "forceful and mandatory" to describe their preferred scrum implementation, and when contributing to online discussion forums Sutherland has used the term "wishy-washy" to disregard current scrum implementations that do not take this forceful approach. It is difficult to speak up in opposition to the founder of a movement, especially when the espoused ideas appear so compelling. Jeff Sutherland is smart, experienced and well respected, but on this issue I feel a sense of discomfort and thus a need to challenge the concept. Is "hyper-productive" what we are seeking? What does that mean anyway? It sounds silver, and bullet-shaped.

What Sutherland and Downey are describing is forced compliance to a process. Is that what scrum is? I don't think so. It isn't what I seek. It isn't the reason I joined this gang. What happened to engagement, to choice, to innovation, to collaboration? Is all of that now discarded as wishy-washy, relegated to the dreaded realm of touchy-feely? What does this mean?

[1] Jeff Sutherland, Scott Downey and Björn Granvik, "Shock Therapy: A Bootstrap for Hyper-Productive Scrum," presented at the Agile 2009 Conference.

I fear the concept of hyper-productivity, represented by shock therapy, will run roughshod over the essential human values of enjoyment and passion, and the empowering feeling of self-organization fueled by trust. And this concerns me.

I am not doing what I do for the sake of hyper-productivity; I am doing it for the sake of freedom, for the sake of advocacy, for a sense of ownership and a sense of self. I guess one could argue that Downey's approach might lead to such empowerment, over time. I have heard that argument before, many years ago: happy people don't produce good software; the act of producing good software makes people happy. The idea has merit, on the surface, but I didn't believe it then, and I don't believe it now. I have not seen it bear fruit, and I think it is a temporary solution. A quick fix. People are worth more than compliance to process.

My feeling, my core belief, is that change has to begin within the individual for it to have any true meaning and long-term sustainability, for it to really matter. Trouble is, I have no metrics to prove this. Sutherland and Downey have metrics. My gut tells me they are questionable metrics, but I am hard-pressed to find a coherent argument to sustain an opposing viewpoint. Process metrics are simple; people metrics (ones that represent the real truth of feeling) are harder to uncover.

I could be completely wrong here, but I don't feel like standing by and letting shock therapy become the default way forward for scrum. Empathy and compassion as agents of change need an advocate too. I'll be that advocate.

The term "Shock therapy" has its roots in the field of psychiatry and while offering some drastic improvement in cases of severe depression and suicidal ideation, it has not been so successful in other situations. It was used between the 1940s and 1980s to "cure" drug addicts, with limited success, and today a gentler, more spiritual approach prevails in the addiction treatment community. It takes longer, but yields a more effective and longer-term recovery. It is altogether kinder. It is curious that such an outmoded approach is seen to be useful in an organizational development context, where we are trying to change a mindset. Will violence really effect such change? I think not.

Based on my understanding of Downey and Sutherland's work I am not encouraged to employ shock therapy as a transformational method, preferring instead to seek a more human and less mechanical approach. Change is so vital to the technology industry that it cannot possibly be represented by process alone.

September 15th, 2008

Software Artisans

Since becoming a software developer somewhat late in life, I have found myself uncomfortable with idea of software developers being thought of as engineers. To me, the creation of software feels more like an artistic endeavor, fulfilling my need for a creative outlet in the way others may take up embroidery, poetry, or watercolor. These thoughts were recently echoed by the well-known usability engineer, Jared Spool, writing in the Agile Usability forum:

> *Something the usability/user experience community isn't addressing is how much this is a craft, where individual prowess trumps collective wisdom and process. We keep wanting to pretend what we do is an engineering discipline, but unfortunately, it's a craft where the skill of the craftsperson dictates success. This is the big elephant in the room that no-one is talking about.*[1]

Reading Spool's remarks prompted me to revisit this discomfort and seek its cause.

I'm guessing that back in the days when the computer revolution began, certain people involved thought that what they were doing was so vitally important to the world (and arguably, it is) that they needed to be recognized as equals to architects, bridge builders, transportation designers, and assorted machine builders. Or—and perhaps more likely—those in academia, or those not doing the work, but profiting from it, established that

[1] Jared Spool, Agile Usability Yahoo Group, January 10, 2006

designation on their behalf. Reading Steven Levy's *Hackers*[2] would indicate this latter supposition to be more likely.

As a result, the entire computer industry attempted to follow what they believed to be "good engineering practices," which led, inevitably, to the world of waterfall development as we know it. So my conclusion here is that a misguided attempt to establish computer programming as a serious discipline, to force-fit the work into an engineering paradigm rather than embrace it as a craft, has caused many of the problems in the world of software development that we, as agilists, are now trying to fix. Pure conjecture on my part, of course, but perhaps not too far from reality.

Crafts, by their nature, are emergent and adaptive, while engineering practices are far less so. Craftsmen continuously inspect and adapt, refine, collaborate, talk to customers, and socialize their skills and knowledge. Such qualities are inherent in the term "craft." Engineers need a more formal, defined approach. Bridges don't really emerge—and those that do will probably, very quickly submerge!

I hope that in twenty years' time, software craftsmen and craftswomen the world over will look back and laugh at us, and at our desperate need to define processes, and invent metrics, and then (finally) to impose "agile" practices on a craft that, really, at its heart, was agile all along. It was just that the vast majority of the people working in the industry didn't know it. It stared us in the face, but our desire for order and repeatability, and to some extent our inflated sense of self-importance as pioneers of a (still) new industry, got in the way, and blocked our vision.

Perhaps the really important thing we'll remember about the

[2] Steven Levy, *Hackers: Heroes of the Computer Revolution* (New York: Anchor Press/Doubleday, 1984)

agile movement is that it allowed us to discover our essential humility, and to feel comfortable with it. I hope so.

December 31, 2005

Distributed Teams are Not Teams

Many scrum practitioners these days are working hard to come up with the best way to make scrum work in distributed (usually off-shore) environments. There are many articles being written on this topic, and many submissions being made to the major scrum and agile conferences. They all say something similar: "We know that co-location is ideal, but the reality is..." They then go on to offer "solutions" (read work-arounds) for the non-ideal, real world situation wherein team members are scattered around the globe.

I find it interesting how the phrase "the real world" is used almost as a weapon to wield against the idealist: Yes, it is all very well to say that teams should be co-located, but that is not how people actually work in the real world. We seem to forget that reality is not something that is imposed on us. Reality isn't just there—we create it. The phrase "the real world" is akin to the phrase "it's just the way we do things around here." Both should be confronted with a healthy dose of skepticism and a steady barrage of "why" questions. Just because it is, doesn't mean it has to be.

Distributed teams are not teams; they are at best a collection of people who communicate regularly. [1] But communication is

[1] I am essentially referring to the off-shoring model, where cheap labor in third world countries is sought, creating dis-located teams, unable to collaborate in any meaningful way. There are exceptions to the distributed team model, where individual (and usually very experienced) developers live far apart, but within a reasonable time-zone difference (i.e. 3 hours maximum) and use practices like remote pairing to ensure high collaboration. I've seen and heard of this working well, but even with this model we lose the "whole team"

not collaboration; it is a poor relation, feeble and flat in comparison. A distributed team cannot create the kind of energy that comes from human eye contact, from shared spontaneous laughter, from physical touch. True collaboration requires all five senses, not just a voice over the telephone or a second-hand video image. And email... don't even go there! Distributed teams require coordination and management and thus can never be truly self-organizing. Time differences and delayed response times inevitably slow down conversation, hold up decisions and ultimately cripple agility. Distributed teams can never be truly agile. So let's stop pretending.

Step back for a moment, and rather than assume we have to take scrum to anyone who asks for it, let's look at an alternative. Try a thought experiment: If all scrum coaches refused to work with organizations that insist on having distributed teams, what would happen? My guess is that those companies would continue to struggle, and many would go under. These companies are requesting scrum exactly because they are struggling, yet they are rarely willing to remodel themselves in an agile way. They want it all: cheap labor and high yield. Not so different from third world child labor industries. Maybe we should simply say no. No, we are not going to support this madness. Force-fitting scrum into such environments may keep them afloat a little longer, but ultimately they are headed for failure. The model is ugly and undignified; it undermines human relationships and is arguably abusive—and from a purely business-focused perspective, it is simply sub-optimal.

Scrum promotes fast failure. Our job as agilists should be to speed up the failure of the distributed team model, not to prolong its agony. Once the organizations that support this

dynamic, where the whole becomes greater than the sum of its parts. In almost all distributed models, we will have only the parts, and as excellent as each part may be, collectively they will still fall short of the synergy created by the whole. On the flip side, it is also important to add that co-location doth not an agile team make. Much more than physical presence is required. It is merely a recommended starting point.

unfortunate model are dead, we can begin building new kinds of companies, flexible, loosely managed, creative companies modeled on true agile principles—ideal ones, not half-hearted ones. The sooner that happens the better. There are many examples of organizations that embrace co-location, self-organization and democracy, and have measurable success to show that this works. Menlo Innovations,[2] the General Electric plant in Durham, NC,[3] and the Brazilian company Semco[4] offer us some interesting case studies to investigate this approach, but ultimately we need to embrace the principles, and not simply take a copy-cat approach.

July 18th, 2008

[2] "Kind of like Kindergarten," *Baltimore Sun,*, July 16, 2008
[3] Charles Fishman, "Engines of Democracy," *Fast Company*, October, 1999
[4] Simon Caulkin, "Who's in charge here? No one," *The Observer*, April 26, 2003

With Great Power...

I had the privilege, recently, of working with an organization in the UK whose managers take scrum seriously and understand that it is more than a quick fix. The director/VP-level management realized that it would take time for scrum to show benefit and, more importantly, they understand the need to trust their development teams.

I spent five days with the company, which committed 25 developers and testers to working full time with me during those five days. That is a big investment, and I recall with dismay those companies where a manager has told me "we can't afford the time to send our employees on a (two-day) learning course—we have work to do," bringing to mind the lumberjack who complains his saw is blunt, but then says he is too busy cutting the tree down to stop and sharpen it. But these UK guys were different.

This company's teams had been doing scrum for about two to three months. The one scrum master they had in place had taken a two-day introductory workshop that I co-facilitated earlier in the year. The teams had seen some success with the transition, but had also started to run aground, and recognized the need for additional support in the form of on-site coaching—a good thing to recognize. I wonder how many companies fail to make that connection and continue to struggle. Scrum is not easy; it surfaces problems and makes things look ugly. Some companies will do their best to hide the unsightly things and plod on with a "hybrid scrum" (eek!) that doesn't address, or even acknowledge, the root causes. Other companies will abandon scrum altogether and reach the conclusion that "agile doesn't work for us." Happily, this UK company decided to go to the next level and work through the difficulties.

The first two days were focused on fostering a shared understanding of the philosophy and framework of scrum. There was a lot of skepticism among the workers—remember this came as a management initiative, not a grassroots one. Most of the skepticism was of the healthy kind (willing to learn) but not all of it. Still, the general mood of the group was positive. My co-facilitator, Michael James, and I were able to make many inroads in creating a shared understanding of the nuts and bolts of scrum, and the use of simple tools such as the physical workflow board—which I more and more see as a core element of a highly functioning scrum team. When used correctly the workflow board will keep a team focused and grounded.

Over the latter three days the work was focused on improving the quality of the product backlog, identifying organizational impediments, and, most interestingly, exploring the limits of self-organization. The outcome was that the teams completely restructured themselves, and removed a "control" group who were responsible for decision making, prioritization, estimation and work assignment. All duties of this control group would now be distributed between teams and product owners. Making these decisions created a feeling of empowerment and freedom among the team members, up to the point where I grew slightly concerned. I sensed a danger that it could move towards a state of anarchy. Could this be too much freedom, too much power? How would it be used?

I recalled the advice Spiderman received from his uncle: "With great power comes great responsibility." The teams were empowered—what, now, was their responsibility? This led to a discussion on responsibility and commitment. The whole group worked on creating a team charter that expressed their commitment to the organization. This was done in small teams, through three iterations, sharing the results with the whole group at the end of each iteration, reconceiving, and then fine-tuning during the subsequent iteration. In this way, we followed a sort of scaled scrum model: living the principles. At the end of the third iteration the product was complete. It was not perfect, but it was a working agreement that everyone present (including the skeptics) felt able to commit to for the next thirty days, when it would be up for review. The team charter would be printed large and displayed around the building for all to see.

Here is a copy of the finished work:

Team Charter

Framework: *We commit to following agile principles to the best of our ability using the whole scrum framework.*

Quality: *We commit to building quality into our products at every stage of their development and to continuously review and improve our techniques for achieving this.*

People: *We are professionals and have a responsibility to respect each other, act honestly, communicate openly and assist/seek assistance where appropriate.*

Process: *We commit to working with the organization to define a minimal process to guide our activities over the duration of each sprint, empowering teams to get the job done.*

Growth: *As individuals, we commit to enhancing and furthering our knowledge and to share that knowledge, as appropriate, with others at [the company].*

I am deeply impressed by this piece of work, and would love to see more organizations create such a document. To me it showed a seriousness and a dedication rare among grassroots workers in a top-down implementation of scrum.

Regardless of whether the management team support this

effort, the work itself allowed the team members to express their preferred way of working and recognize that they each have a say in their own destiny. Organizational transformation is difficult, but it has to start somewhere and I'm a true believer that the grassroots level of an organization is the best place to begin.

August 2nd, 2006

Unearthing Impediments by Doing Less

It is common for new teams to have difficulty articulating impediments, and for scrum masters to struggle with the kinds of questions they should ask team members in order to identify impediments.

I don't believe it helps to focus on asking questions. I think it more effective to focus on creating an environment of visibility and honesty. Workflow boards help us do that, but workflow boards alone won't achieve it. Sometimes we need a whack to the side of the head.

The biggest impediment I have discovered to identifying impediments is the practice of measuring tasks in hours, and having team members update those hours at each meeting. Fundamentalist scrum practitioners look at me askance when I make that suggestion. It doesn't seem to make sense; but it does.

Some years ago, I took over as scrum master for a team that had been doing scrum "by the book" (their words). All of them hated the standup meetings, and especially the updating of hours. They felt they were being measured at a micro-level, that they should just be trusted to do the work, and that it was insulting and a waste of time to be doing this. Well, being someone inclined to trust gut-feeling over metrics, I was happy to accommodate this request. While adaptations to scrum itself tend to be frowned upon today,[1] back in the early days there was

[1] This has become apparent through the invention of the derogatory term "scrumbut," meaning "We are doing scrum but we don't do X."

more of a culture of experimentation, in the spirit of "inspect and adapt." I figured I was still allowed to call it scrum, which in that particular corporate culture was important.

We agreed that no hours would be put on tasks on the condition that all tasks were considered small enough to be completed in a single day. This latter condition is very important. What we discovered through this process change is that when tasks were not done in one day it was an indication of an impediment that no one had thought to mention, or were even able to acknowledge as an impediment. Now, some of these "impediments" are very tiny, such as "we thought the task was easier," so the solution is to break the task into smaller pieces and commit to a smaller task for the next day, but other impediments that surface in this way can be indicative of a bigger problem.

For example, the teams were falling behind, and one developer had a task sitting in the work-in-progress (WIP) column of the workflow board for three days. After one day, he said it was almost done and just a bit bigger than he'd thought. We marked it with a red spot (this red-spot marking gives an immediate visual indication of the blocked tasks). After two days, he said he didn't have time to complete it. That raised some eyebrows. Why not? It turned out that this particular developer was frequently being called away to fix bugs in another property. This had nothing to do with the project he was on, and had not been discussed in the planning meeting. No one on the team had viewed this as an impediment because "that's just the way we do things round here." Clearly, something needed to change.

This issue would not have come to the surface so quickly if we hadn't had the "one-day task" rule. The process of measuring things at a micro-level, with the intent of creating visibility, actually serves to obfuscate important information.

I recall another team I worked with (one using an electronic tool to track tasks) where the developers would knock hours off all the tasks they were working on, even if they knew they hadn't done much work on them. They were all keen to see the burndown chart actually burn down, and didn't feel safe saying the size of the task was the same or bigger. By the end of the sprint almost all tasks had about one hour remaining. Very few were done—and no stories were done. This convinced me of the need for binary measurement. A task is either done or not done. A task with one hour remaining is not done.

Having this team stop measuring partially done work and measure only completed things (tasks and stories) helped them to better understand what they could realistically commit to, and simultaneously created an environment of honesty and trust. It also allowed the impediments that were preventing them from completing tasks to be identified much faster (usually in 24 hours or less).

Since 2005 I have discouraged all teams I work with from measuring and tracking in hours. Using the "one-day task" rule will very quickly uncover impediments and dysfunction. It will also free up your developers to actually focus on the work, and off the numbers. The ultimate goal is to take focus off the tasks altogether, and focus on the actual request. Tasks in themselves have zero value; they are only steps on the journey. The story, or request, is the artifact of true interest to the customer.

Scrum requires a massive shift in thinking and behaving. Freeing yourself of the notion that measuring in hours is somehow necessary or useful will be a great leap towards your agile edge.

June 23rd, 2009

Test(osterone)-Infected Developers

Men are from Development, women are from Testing. Not intended as an aggravating, politically-incorrect statement, but an observation. I have worked with many software companies over the years, and inevitably in each company the proportion of women to men is far greater in testing (aka Quality Assurance, or QA) than it is in development. Why is that? What is it about testing that attracts female techies, or an equally valid question, what is it about development that repels them? Well, I have my theories.

In traditional software environments, development departments are frequently characterized by hero-behavior, by machismo, by one-upmanship, and are fueled by promotional desires which provide a level of self-importance, over-lording, and maybe even a window cube. It is often about ego, bluster and winning, and the energy is just... very male. One rarely sees a woman thrive in such an environment. Often she takes a backseat in decision making, follows rather than leads, and relinquishes responsibility; not always, but often. Some women do rise to management positions in development departments. They are usually tough managers! There is almost a sense that they have to be tougher than their male counterparts to survive. Female development managers are the exception that proves the rule.

And then there's this: The discipline of testing requires a lot more humility than the discipline of development. Testers tend to be more humble than developers; it is the nature of the role.

There are different energies at play: development is characterized by the energy of creation, testing by the energy of service. Women traditionally gravitate towards the latter.

The way traditional software environments work, testing follows development. Interesting how in traditional paternalistic societies women follow men. What does that say about our corporate cultures?

The mission of scrum is to change the way we work. This is not process change, this is culture change. People inside a scrum/agile process (we hope) behave differently. We now have test-infected developers. That's great. We have developers who see the value in testing, and do it. They don't push it off to QA people at the end of the process. So where does that leave the tester? I'll turn to three women for the answer. Abby Fichner addresses this question in her 2009 essay on agile testing,[1] and I quote:

> *Testers can work with customers up front, before a feature has been developed. They can dig beyond the stated requirement to learn what it will take for the feature to actually be usable. The criteria by which users will judge it. In the end, success is defined by the software's usefulness to the user, not by its adherence to documents. And so if testers are going to have to figure out how to validate that it meets those user needs, why not figure that out up front—and allow that knowledge to help drive development in the right direction? The truth is, it's a waste of testers' skills and an exercise in frustration to leave them until the end—trying to inject quality into something that's already built.*

Lisa Crispin and Janet Gregory have written extensively about the tester's role on an agile team.[2] They define an agile tester as:

[1] Abby Fichner, "Where Do the Testers Go In Agile?" *The Hacker Chick Blog* (thehackerchickblog.com), June 2009

[2] Lisa Crispin and Janet Gregory, *Agile Testing: A Practical Guide for Testers and Agile Teams*, (Boston: Addison-Wesley Professional, 2009)

> *...a professional tester who embraces change, collaborates well with both technical and business people, and understands the concept of using tests to document requirements and drive development. Agile testers tend to have good technical skills, know how to collaborate with others to automate tests, and are also experienced exploratory testers. They're willing to learn what customers do so that they can better understand the customers' software requirements.*

What is being described here is something quite alien to the end-of-process, follow-the-plan testers many of us have worked with—the people that simply gate-keep for sloppy developers.

We have been quick to acknowledge the new term, "test-infected developer," but what should we call the testing counterpart? Development-infected tester seems an intuitive choice, but it's inadequate. This is not about writing code, so that term doesn't reach where I want this to go. I prefer the term "creation-infected testers." I want to see testers passionate about creating new software, not just validating someone else's software. I want to see testers weave themselves into the creative process, from requirements all the way through to release—weave and be woven. It is time to embrace the quieter, more intuitive voice. We need to move away from the entrenched pattern of testers supporting developers—women supporting their men. We need to seek equality in our software relationships as we seek equality in our marriages.

Women need to claim their rightful place in the creation process. Agile environments (and agile environmentalists) will create the space for that to occur, but it is up to the individuals to move into that space, either as test-infected developers, or creation-infected testers, or simply as artisans. The time is now.

June 25th, 2009

Paying Off Technical Debt

...the agile movement has focused on high levels of customer involvement—basically a good thing—but we've gone too far. A large number of Agilists decry that they can't get organizations to focus on technical practices—but why should that be a surprise when we encourage product managers/owners to make all the priority decisions and then measure performance using velocity?[1]

This passage by Jim Highsmith brought to mind an experience I had a few years ago, when working as a scrum master/coach with a team in New York City. This is how they handled technical excellence, and debt:

1. When a team member came across badly written, irrelevant, or messy code (including code written without unit tests) during an iteration, they didn't fix it—unless it was crucial to writing the code necessary for the feature they were working on at that time. Instead they noted the file, line numbers and feature/s that it touched and added a sticky note (or several) to a boxed-out section of the workflow board labeled, suitably, "Technical Debt." Then they continued meeting their commitment for the sprint.

2. During any sprint planning meeting, when a request was made for a feature, at least one team member (usually more, as they were all active in reading these notes) now knew if there were any danger-areas in the code for that feature. This would be mentioned and discussed, and the estimate increased accordingly. The team had a policy (agreed upon with management)

[1] Jim Highsmith, "Velocity is Killing Agility!", *jimhighsmith.com*, November 2, 2011

to never add more debt. Coding around existing problems adds debt, and thus increases the interest on that debt, ultimately leading to technical bankruptcy.

3. If the product owner still wanted the feature, the team would add all the technical debt sticky notes as tasks for that story, and repair the code before/during the creation of that feature. Needless to say, brand new features were coded to the standards of excellence the team had set themselves.

This simple process made the code quality highly visible to all. Even without technical knowledge a simple count of sticky notes told a story, and everyone wanted the count to go down. It allowed developers to produce evidence for any higher-than-expected estimations; and perhaps most importantly, created an open, value-oriented dialog between developers and business.

I have introduced this technique to many teams since, but no other team (that I know of) has taken up the practice. It isn't easy, but I'd say it is essential to put this, or a similar mechanism in place to create healthy dialog and avoid the pitfalls Jim Highsmith mentions in his article. The problem isn't using velocity as a measure (that can be useful if applied appropriately), nor is it having the business make the priority decisions (they ought to!) The problem—as always—is the absence of true collaborative dialog, without which people are likely to be uninformed, to make assumptions and to have unrealistic expectations.

February 12th, 2012

The Agile Explorer

While consulting in Indianapolis, I had a conversation with a developer, who opened with, "What do you know about nuclear power?" He went on to inform me that he'd worked in a nuclear power plant, and then told me all plant workers are trained continually on safety procedures, even if they are seasoned veterans of a plant. Keeping people refreshed with current thinking and frequent reminders of good practice, he said, helps ensure against a meltdown. He asked why it was that agile training tended to be a one-shot deal. His own observations at various companies attempting an agile transformation was that that people started out doing well after a training, full of newly acquired knowledge and enthusiasm, but this energy would quickly deteriorate as people fell back into old behavior. "Software companies melt down too," he said.

This got me thinking about the solutions companies adopt to introduce and manage scrum. They usually engage short-term consultants and/or trainers. The more committed hire scrum masters, usually seeking someone who had been certified by one of the ever-growing number of certification bodies, as if this is some guarantee of greatness. Both approaches barely scratch the surface.

I am periodically concerned that the very term "scrum master" has held back the agile movement, and that the role itself is an impediment to self-organization. While the intent is noble, the role as it is played out in practice too often becomes that of a metrics gatherer and process enforcer, or at worst, a scrum policeman, or even an "agile project manager." When this happens, responsibility is wrested from the team members, who become disengaged and subservient to a process that feels enforced and thrust upon them.

In the past two years I have found myself talking less and less about the scrum master role as I teach scrum. I frame scrum as a relationship between product owner and team, and explore that relationship in terms of team culture, focus, alignment and collaboration. This is the promise of scrum: engaged teams and delighted customers. But this approach doesn't solve the meltdown problem—it doesn't help the organization move to a sustainable model of continual improvement around the foundational principles and framework of scrum.

Hiring scrum masters is not the answer. They are always low on the hierarchical totem pole, often answerable to a project management office or development director. They have little autonomy and frequently fall into complicity with the existing status quo.

I don't believe agile coaching is the answer either. Coaching can help individuals and teams self-actualize. But as with therapy, there comes a time when the coachee needs to move on, or risk going round in circles with the coach and building an unhealthy, co-dependent relationship. What we really need is to get agile into the very DNA of an organization. We know we can change an organism's current DNA by introducing a virus, a virus strong enough to fight off the antibodies of the host organism and thrive. If we are going to shift organizational culture, we need to plant a virus in that organization.

I'd like to propose a new role for organizations—a viral agent: The agile explorer. This, to be clear, is nothing like an "agile champion," who is usually the CEO or VP of Development, the person who says, "Let's go agile!" but who doesn't necessarily get the organizational transformation this requires, nor has the time to commit to true change.

The agile explorer, our agent of change, is one who seeks

knowledge and journeys into unchartered territory. He/she is a dreamer and a fearless adventurer who, through action, inspires others to journey alongside. The agile explorer is a full-time role, and should ideally report to no one, but if reporting is essential, then to the CEO in a non-performance-measured, autonomous role. This person is not there to coach teams, or to help people get better at scrum. He/she is there to listen, think, inspire, confront, agitate, challenge, and open the collective organizational eyes to new possibilities, seeding new ways of being.

A good agile explorer will be engaged in the wider agile community, attend events, join online discussion forums, read extensively, learn new ideas, create dialogs in conversation with other organizations and individuals, establish in-house talks and workshops, generate ideas around experimental improvement, and—perhaps most importantly— encourage others to do the same.

The agile explorer will weave silos and hierarchies into stunning works of kinetic art, creating a sense of awe and wonder. In such an environment self-organization will flourish, peer coaching will emerge as an alternative to expensive, uninvested hired hands, engagement will deepen, delight will increase—and meltdown will be averted, one inspired day at a time.

April 19th, 2012

Heartfelt Emotionalism is the New Hardcore

I am often described as "touchy-feely" in my approach to teaching agile. This term is almost always used as an insult, and while I can take it with a pinch of salt, the fear and ignorance behind such a statement inevitably makes me sad. I find that too many people throw out that term to describe ways of human engagement they don't really understand—and this seems to be especially true in the software world. It is a way of making light of a form of interaction that many software engineers and related folk find very difficult. Dismissing such interaction as "touchy-feely" or "soft" is a way of avoiding it. Quite simply, it is a cop-out.

Our industry harbors a perception that ordering people around, setting schedules, micro-directing, threatening people with demotion and termination and generally being fierce is a hardcore approach to management, while the approach of listening, trusting, fostering healthy dialog, promoting self-organization and resolving conflicts is considered soft. How topsy-turvy! It is surely the other way around.

Command-and-control management is fear-based management. The approach is all bluster and no courage. There is nothing "hard" about it; indeed its resulting ineffectiveness show it to be utterly flaccid and sadly impotent.

My colleague, the improv teacher and performer, Matt Smith, says about his improvisation exercises, "Nothing soft here; this is the hard stuff—this takes real courage." Working successfully with people is immensely challenging and tough. This is not touchy-feely, this is heartfelt emotionalism. This is not soft-skills, this is hardcore.

The scrum mindset requires us to challenge every single assumption we have ever had about the way we do our work. If you find yourself using the term "touchy-feely" when things get uncomfortable, or describing human relationship-building as soft, please stop for a moment and reflect on your motives. Are you hiding? Are you embarrassed? Are you afraid? Be honest. Chances are that's exactly what is happening. Reframe your statement, and begin to appreciate how warm, kind—even loving—personal relationships underlie all successful teamwork, and thus all successful product creation. Recognize that building such relationships takes immense courage.

Come on, get in touch with your heartfelt emotionalism—be hardcore!

June 14th, 2009

The People's Scrum

In the many years I have been teaching and promoting scrum, I have rejected the idea that scrum is a methodology, or a process, and socialized the concept of scrum as a framework for unearthing organizational dysfunction and empowering individuals toward a new way of thinking about work: Scrum as a force for change. More recently (and it seems to coincide with the rise of kanban) I have heard increasing talk of both kanban and scrum being described as tools, e.g. Kanban vs. Scrum.[1] This concerns me.

I have nothing against tools. When I facilitate workshops, or work inside organizations as a scrum consultant, I often teach people the art of relative estimation, and in the process may introduce Planning Poker™, a card game for team estimation designed by Mike Cohn. Planning Poker™ is a tool. The "As a.../I want.../so that...." story template, also designed by Cohn, is another tool.[2] Likewise, a talking stick in a stand up meeting, a timeline in a retrospective, and various other techniques we employ to effectively do our work can be considered tools of the trade. But scrum itself is not a tool. Scrum is a way of thinking about how we do our work, it is a state of mind, a journey, an exploration of self and environment. To reduce it to "a tool" is to completely miss its magic and bring us back into a world of best practices and repeatable process. No, this isn't a big leap. Consider it.

It saddens me to see so many agilists refer to scrum as "just

[1] Henrik Kniberg, *Kanban vs. Scrum: Making the Best of Both* (Toronto: InfoQ Mini-Books, 2009)
[2] Mike Cohn, *Agile Estimation and Planning* (New Jersey: Prentice Hall, 2005)

another tool" and somehow interchangeable with kanban, or even XP. Perhaps kanban is a tool, one that is used for process efficiency—essentially value stream measurement and improvement. Its biggest proponent in the agile world, David Anderson, refers to it as a process, but I can see it both ways. XP, like scrum, has the potential to foster heartfelt change, as it offers a set of values to incorporate in our working lives, but due to its strong programming focus is more often understood as a set of engineering practices and tools (pair programming, test-driven development, continuous integration, etc.). It is rarely used in the holistic way it was designed. Perhaps, just as with scrum, truly embracing XP is beyond the average person's comfort zone.

The other direction I see scrum heading toward is that of becoming a "best practice." I feel uneasy when I see Jeff Sutherland attempt to align scrum with CMMi.[3] I am not opposed to this (not yet), and I am hoping to learn more about the direction Jeff and others are going in, but I am wary. I feel it is movement towards hyper-productivity, big profits and ultra-efficiency, and thus away from the joy of work. I am a strong believer in business value and profit growing from a sense of love and satisfaction for what we do, from care and passion, not from being streamlined and made hyper- or ultra- anything. I want to see The People's Scrum, not the VC's Scrum, or the CEO's Scrum, or the Consultant's Scrum. I believe only The People's Scrum is sustainable and true.

The People's Scrum is scrum created by the people for the people, not scrum as dictated by a book or a training course or a consultant. The People's Scrum grows organically through education, practice, failure and reflection. I welcome the mixed messages the various scrum practitioners send forth, all the disagreements and arguments on the lists and blogs. The knowledge work industry is a quagmire, a tangled mess, and teams

[3] Jeff Sutherland, Carsten Ruseng Jakobsen, Kent Johnson, "Scrum and CMMI Level 5: The Magic Potion for Code Warriors," presented at the Agile 2007 Conference

working in collaboration and accord need to find their own way through this—people helping people. It will take a while, and is perhaps a never-ending journey. But it's *our* journey—our adventure.

Scrum is a framework for organizational change and personal freedom. It is not a methodology, it is not a process, and it is much more than a tool. Scrum dares us to think about the world in an utterly new and different way. We must learn to stop mapping and to start drawing in wild colors and crazy patterns onto blank sheets of paper. Then we might start to get this.

December 6th, 2009

Process

The Ragged Pathway

Process is simply "the way we do things." An agile process is always emergent. It is never prescribed. Agile is about release—letting go and trusting. It is about stripping away the nonsense, the waste, and creating space for people to think for themselves, to create new rhythms, new forms of collaboration, to confront and explore rather than comply and execute. A key principle of any agile method is learning, often framed as inspect/adapt. If we don't begin by doing things, however clumsily, we'll have nothing to inspect. Thus an agile process requires action—and frequently it requires failure.

Scrum: Its Place in the World

Scrum is not some newfangled, flash-in-the pan framework for software development. The whole agile movement is a very small part of a greater movement in the business world, and perhaps the world of organizations in general. We are at the beginning of a true Kuhnian paradigm shift[1] away from a mechanistic way of thinking and toward a human one, a living one. The theory underlying this worldview is known as complexity science, and in particular the study of complex adaptive systems (CAS).[2] A book that does an excellent job of discussing this shift of thinking and behaving in the business world—one I recommend to upper managers and change agents in the organizations I work with—is *Surfing the Edge of Chaos*[3] by Richard Pascale, Mark Milleman and Linda Gioja. The authors offer advice to business leaders on how to turn their companies into "agile and adaptable 'living systems' that achieve long-term vitality and sustainability in a swiftly evolving environment." The book is peppered with real-life examples of major business entities

[1] The term "paradigm shift" was introduced by Thomas Kuhn in his 1962 book, *The Structure of Scientific Revolutions*. Kuhn argues that scientific advancement is not evolutionary, but rather is a "series of peaceful interludes punctuated by intellectually violent revolutions," and in those revolutions "one conceptual world view is replaced by another." Kuhn asserted that once the new paradigm is in place, there is absolutely no room for the old paradigm. Thomas S. Kuhn, *The Structure of Scientific Revolutions*, (Chicago: Univ. of Chicago Press, 1962)

[2] John H. Miller and Scott E. Page, *Complex Adaptive Systems: An Introduction to Computational Models of Social Life*, (New Jersey: Princeton University Press, 2007)

[3] Richard T. Pascale, Mark Milleman and Linda Gioja, *Surfing the Edge of Chaos: The Laws of Nature and the New Laws of Business* (New York: Crown Business, 2001)

(e.g. Shell and Sears) who have harnessed complex, adaptive behaviors for profit and employee happiness.

One organization dedicated to promoting these ideas is the Plexus Institute,[4] which offers the best explanation I have yet read of what complex adaptive systems are, and what they signify:

> *What is complexity science? Very simply, it is science's most recent attempt to explain how order and novelty emerge in the world. (As such it is the intellectual successor to systems theory and chaos theory.) The traditional view of the natural world was made up of machine-like entities that you could understand by taking them apart and examining the components.*
>
> *Much has been learned about nature by this approach. But the vast majority of nature is not amenable to being understood in this way, because most of nature is made up of what complexity scientists call non-linear, complex adaptive systems. Such systems are created by a number of diverse and independent agents that are constantly changing and interacting with each other. In complex adaptive systems, a study of the parts surely produces an incomplete understanding of the whole. Examples of these systems include ant colonies, ecosystems, and human organizations.*
>
> *It's worth making a distinction here between complex and complicated. An internal combustion engine is complicated, with many different components. But it is not complex because knowing what the parts are and how they function permits you to know what the system as a whole does.*

The institute's online literature goes on to point out that "Such understandings give us powerful new ways of thinking about and acting on issues which span human concern, from such

[4] plexusinstitute.org

seemingly disparate domains as ecological preservation, childhood education and executive leadership."

The forward-thinking people at the Plexus Institute may be aware of the agile movement—certainly their frame of reference seems broad enough that they probably are, but as systems scientists, they are concerned with systems in general, and not something as narrow as profit-making organizations. Their description of what they call the "defining feature of complex adaptive systems," is very in tune with an enlightened agilist's understanding of his craft:

> *...the order that emerges through the interactions of components in complex systems is "greater than—and different from—the sum of the parts," to use a familiar phrase. Complex systems therefore have a large degree of unpredictability. But more than that, the emergent collective order in turn influences the behavior, or interactions, of the parts. Feedback loops exist at every level. Such systems are constantly adapting and evolving... the order of the whole system flows from distributed control, that is from interactions among individuals, not from central control. In organizations, one way to think about this phenomenon, called self-organization, is to remember what happens in times of crisis. People take on tasks where they see the need, often breaking the normal rules of operation, often doing things they don't normally do. People achieve amazing feats, which they often rank among the most rewarding experiences of their work lives. Leaders often find it difficult to give up a measure of control, because it is part of their identity as leaders. But those who do find that their people tap into their latent talent, and do far more than they, or anyone, ever imagined. This is the power of a complexity perspective in organizations.*

This perspective does not say that leaders simply have to sit back, give up control, and wait for unpredictable miracles. Instead, it argues that leaders must help create conditions that unleash the talent distributed among their people. It is a model of leader as cultivator rather than controller.

My intention here (using mostly borrowed words) is to show that agile is a naturally evolving way of thinking and behaving. It has a solid theoretical and scientific foundation and is at the cutting edge of current systems thinking. As such, agile needs to be taken very seriously by any software company hoping to stay in business and compete in a world that is changing faster than ever before. Mechanics cannot keep up; heavy-handed, hierarchical, command-driven organizations are the lumbering dinosaurs of the business world, grinding innovation to a halt. To thrive today we need a light, hands-off approach to management. We need to surrender to chaos, and harness change to our advantage. We need to embrace the innate creativity of the human mind, to trust and release people into the solution space. And we need to create systems and foster environments within which people can excel.

All of this requires a personal paradigm shift. We cannot force fit this new way of working into our old way of thinking. Something will break. Since I have used so many of the Plexus Institute's words in this essay, it seems only fitting I should give them the last word:

> *One final property of complex adaptive systems that is relevant to organizations is as follows: when the interactions among the agents are enhanced, the adaptability and creativity of the system is also enhanced.*
>
> *In human organizations, this translates to agents being people, and interactions being relationships generated by conversations. Enhancing people's ability to interact and to develop enhances the adaptability of the organization. Complexity scientists have also observed that a diversity of agents in the system serves to enhance this adaptability and creativity even*

further. In organizations, this means inviting a diversity of experience and perspectives." [5]

September 26th, 2008

[5] "The Plexus Story," plexusinstitute.org

When is Scrum Not Scrum?

In teaching scrum and working with organizations in a consulting/coaching capacity I have found more and more that some of the practices as outlined in the two original scrum books, *Agile Software Development with Scrum* by Ken Schwaber and Mike Beedle and *Agile Project Management with Scrum* by Schwaber alone,[1, 2] are outdated and unhelpful. I teach what I know works and what I see as being appropriate. This differs slightly in each context, but I have found certain practices to be effective, all of which differ from standard scrum practices. Some would be considered radically different, which leads to the difficult question, the title of this essay: when is scrum not scrum? [3]

1. Product owners are part of the team

Having a hard separation between PO and team is unhelpful; it causes rifts and exacerbates the "them and us" culture. I discarded the distasteful "pigs and chickens" terminology a long time ago, and now encourage teams to incorporate the product representative (not owner) into the daily meetings and the retrospective as well as the planning and review meetings. To do this successfully requires a different mindset from everyone

[1] Ken Schwaber and Mike Beedle, *Agile Software Development with Scrum*, (New Jersey: Prentice Hall, 2001)

[2] Ken Schwaber, *Agile Project Management with Scrum*, (Redmond, Washington: Microsoft Press, 2004)

[3] This essay was written in 2007, and since then the common thinking in the scrum world has grown more aligned with these ideas, e.g. product owners are now considered part of the scrum team, sprints are more likely to be 1-2 weeks rather than 30 days, hours measurement is seen for the waste it is and physical workflow boards have replaced spreadsheets in many organizations. There is still a long way to go, and many practitioners still hang onto scrum as it was first documented. Some people just need prescriptive process.

involved, so the style of training and adoption needs to change accordingly. This is not trivial.

2. One- or two-week sprints

Thirty days for a sprint may have been appropriate twelve years ago when scrum was developed. Today it is far too long. It is also true (from my experience) that teams are incapable of planning a thirty-day sprint effectively. It is overwhelming. Most teams I have tried it with nail the first part of the sprint, but allow the second part to be vague and muddy. They get exhausted by the eight-hour meeting, and simply find the timeframe too long to plan effectively. A thirty day timeframe also means a customer change request can take up to 60 days to be completed; that is far too long.

3. Tasks are not measured in hours

Insisting on an hours breakdown and requiring that each team member continually update hours remaining on a task is often perceived as a sneaky, micro-management approach. In my experience team members find this practice frustrating and meaningless. In 2005 I moved toward encouraging team members to break all tasks down to be as small as possible. A task must be completed in a single working day, or it is considered an impediment, and should be marked as such. This approach serves two purposes: first, ease and accuracy of tracking (i.e. burn down on tasks rather than hours, to make the whole process binary: a task is done or it is not done), and second, it surfaces impediments developers themselves may not see. For example, an incomplete task may be in that state because a developer was called off into some long and meaningless meeting, but because "that's just the way we work around here" this is not seen as an impediment. Physical markers on tasks (e.g. stickers on task cards) show the truth of what is happening. See the essay "Unearthing Impediments By Doing Less" for more on this.

4. Use of workflow boards rather than spreadsheets

The scrum books, and many scrum certification courses, promote the use of spreadsheets or other electronic tools to track the sprint—which is horrible. Spreadsheets hide information, and they lie. The best way to create transparency is to display everything on big visible charts, sometimes known as information radiators. The interactive, collaborative nature of a workflow board lends itself to the scrum process, like no electronic tool ever can. If this idea triggers the question, "how does this work with distributed teams?" I suggest you are asking the wrong question. Scrum is most effective with co-located teams. Ask yourself how you might make that a reality.

5. Backlogs on the wall

Again, a move away from spreadsheets and other electronic tools. At least the next 3-4 sprints' worth of stuff should be displayed on index cards on the wall of the team room so the team can take look-ahead time whenever they need it. Backlogs much longer than that, containing anything more than placeholder items (reminders) can be thought of as wasteful, in any case. The less time we give to thinking ahead—in detail—about features that may never see the light of day, the better.

6. Estimation Meetings

Estimation, interestingly, is less about measurement and more about learning. I think it is good to understand effort, but more useful is to reach a common understanding of the request. Indeed, the former follows the latter. Estimation is done before the first sprint, and then on a regular basis during each sprint. I have found that a 1-2 hour meeting about 2-3 days before the end of a sprint is the ideal time. There are many ways to estimate, and some of these ways are addressed later in other essays. Generally, I find estimation more useful when it is done on a relative scale, e.g. story points, rather than in units of time, e.g.

"ideal developer days" as described in the original scrum books. The estimation meeting is an integral part of a successful cycle. Having the backlog on the wall ensures developers have continual look-ahead time (see point 5, above), thus keeping the estimation meetings short.

7. Insistence on agile engineering practices

It isn't enough to assume that because a team is "doing scrum" that engineering practices will begin to change. They won't. And they don't. It is essential that scrum teams introduce some core practices such as unit testing, early acceptance test specification, componentized design, continuous refactoring and pairing from the start. This doesn't mean the practices can or will all be undertaken immediately, but I cannot overstress the importance of such practices. Scrum itself says nothing about such practices, and that tends to give organizations a sense that scrum is easy to do, and can simply (as many of its proponents state) wrap around existing engineering practices. I have seen this approach fail too often to have any faith that it is true. It is simply counterintuitive.

8. The scrum master role is not always necessary

An effective self-organizing team is exactly that: self-organizing. Leadership emerges from the team when the key agile principles are adhered to. The scrum master role becomes superfluous in a healthy agile organization. There is a role for agile leadership at all levels in an organization, but scrum-mastering is probably not it, being too often viewed as a form of project management—a style used to drive people, rather than serve them. Coaching should be appropriate to the context. I have seen a lot of inexperienced scrum masters fall into old project manager habits, and have seen teams simply accept this lapse, because that is how they are used to working. I also have issues with the term scrum master; language often dictates how we behave, and this term doesn't help to break paradigms.

So is what I offer still scrum? Perhaps it is; there is enough of the original flow there to claim so: planning meeting, daily meetings, delivery of working software each sprint, retrospective—but ultimately the name itself is superfluous. The agility inherent in the principles toward which I teach and coach allows fundamental change to take place in organizations. That is what I am after. If it helps to call it scrum, we can call it scrum. It offends to call it scrum, we can call it something else. Eventually, it will simply be "what we do."

February 21st, 2007

Addition and Subtraction in Scrum

I see two different mindsets in the scrum community. They can be simply expressed as i) scrum is malleable and should be changed when necessary, and ii) scrum is fixed and should stay the same.[1] Members of the group endorsing the first mindset are willing to explore scrum in context, and alter it to fit their purpose. Members of the latter group hold on to the simplicity of scrum as first documented, believing the framework is appropriate in all cases. I have concerns with both mindsets.

There are two ways to embellish scrum; one is to add things; the other is to remove things. Both need to be handled with care. I tend to agree that the simplicity of scrum is its strength, and I'm wary when people say we need to add roles, or define the process more clearly.

On the other hand, I am all for seeking out and removing waste, so if I find that certain practices in "original" scrum don't add value, I will not use them. I found that, for example, with hours-tracking (see also "When is Scrum Not Scrum?" and "Unearthing Impediments by Doing Less"). There are other ways to know if the work is on track for a sprint, simpler ways that require no tracking at all from developers. Anything that allows

[1] E.g. this comment by Dave Barrett, seen on the ScrumDevelopment Yahoo! Group, February, 2007: "I think that the book [*Agile Software Development with Scrum*] is just as relevant today as it was when Ken wrote it. We still use 30 day Sprints, an Excel spreadsheet for burndown charts, track in hours and estimate in Ideal Developer days. And it works just fine thank you. I think I understand why people feel the need to embellish scrum: it's just too simple. However, it doesn't need embellishment, and keeping focused on the basics is probably the key to success."

a developer to be free to create seems like a value-add. The responsibility for updating work is still there, the commitment to completion is still there, the process is just much simpler.

The danger of this "stripping away" approach is that people begin to think along lines like this: "Oh, the daily scrum doesn't add value, it's just a waste of time, let's drop it." Which is a very, very bad idea. So when can a scrum practice be safely dropped? I think the simple answer is: when it is not being dropped to mask a dysfunction. Often, when people decide to drop this or that scrum practice they are not aware that their action may be hiding a real and important issue. This is where experience comes into it. An experienced scrum practitioner can assess the value of a particular practice, weigh it against any downside, such as loss of transparency, and make an informed choice. Every choice of course can be revisited at the next retrospective.

I also see a big difference between dropping scrum practices and breaking the scrum framework, and understanding that difference is also something that comes with experience. When you remove a practice, you can safely do so if you retain the value that practice was providing. As an example, dropping ideal developer days as a measure and not estimating at all may be unwise, but replacing this technique with a relative measure, such as tee-shirt sizing, is smart; it retains the value that estimation provides and brings better opportunity for dialog along with it.

In general I am in favor of simplifying any process, and opposed to making things more complex or worse, more complicated. Adding things to scrum usually results in complication. Removing things can result in simplicity, but only if it is done wisely and with a good understanding of scrum principles and values, otherwise the result will be confusion and a return to whatever was in place before scrum came along (which we can safely assume was not good).

March 3rd, 2007

Estimation

The following three essays on estimation, written in 2007, 2012 and 2010, respectively, all appear to contradict each other. The first one praises size estimation over time estimation, the second promotes the concept of the (clearly time-based) "team day" measure for estimating, and the third decries all estimation. I still stand behind all three ideas; the discerning reader will understand that the contradiction is only apparent, and the three essays actually support the same idea. Estimation can be used as a way of forcing commitment and trying to make "accurate predictions," or it can be used as a way of engaging customers and developers in meaningful dialog. All three essays promote the latter idea. The technique chosen is really immaterial.

Estimation I: Size

It surprises me, but I regularly come across a few people in the agile field who prefer estimating in "actual time" (e.g. hours or days) over estimating in size (e.g. story points). I have even heard statements such as, "The most advanced implementations of agile use actual time estimation, because it offers the most powerful benefits." My gut feeling has always told me otherwise, but I found that I didn't have a well-thought out argument beyond, "Um... read Mike Cohn's book," [1] which in the event of a real-time discussion is not very helpful, and even so does not address all of the arguments I have been hearing against size-based estimation. What follows is my attempt to clarify my own thoughts on this matter. I focus on four specific arguments in favor of time measurement and attempt to counter those arguments.

Argument #1: Estimating in hours allows a developer to measure his estimate against his actual, and use that data to improve his estimates in future.

This is true, and it works very well if a project has only a single developer working on it, or has more than one developer but they are all essentially working alone, on different parts of a system—a common model in a "build-by-layers" approach to system development.

Problems arise, however, when we introduce the concept of cross-functional teams working on transactional "slices" of a system. What is a team-hour? Is it the whole team working for one hour together, or is it the average time it would take one

[1] Mike Cohn, *Agile Estimation and Planning* (New Jersey: Prentice Hall, 2005)

team member to do the work? Already we are beginning to talk in abstract time, not actual time. One team member may be twice as fast as most of the others, through familiarity with the system and/or greater experience; does one hour to him mean the same as it means to the others? Clearly not. "One hour" becomes a confusing unit of measurement in such cases. It is also the case that different team members have different responsibilities. How do we find a unit of time appropriate across documentation, UI design, coding and testing? How does each team member measure the time other team members will take for their part of the work on the story? You'll see that this quickly becomes completely unmanageable.

Some scrum/agile teams use hour estimates at the task level, with the assumption that a single developer will work on each task; this seems reasonable as the tasks are divided across skill boundaries, such as server-side, database, testing, etc. In this case, Argument #1 seems to hold good: developers should estimate in hours at a task level and then improve their estimates by measuring estimates against actuals. Unfortunately, this argument breaks down again as soon as we recognize that the best code creation, and the best testing, is done in pairs. Again, what does one hour mean? Is it a pair-hour or an hour for one of the pair? What if we don't know in advance (as we probably should not) who will pair with whom and on what? Who gives the hour estimates? Everybody? Just one person? If so, which person?

In general, I find the practice of estimating task time to result in massive, wasteful overhead. Tasks should be small; they should move across the task board in a single working day. The focus of estimation should be at the story level, as the story is where the business value lies.

Argument #2: Our customers/product owners don't understand story points; they need to know how many hours developers are working so they know how much the work will cost.

I hope anyone reading this can see the immediate flaw in this argument: micro-management. Product owners and customers have no business knowing how many hours each developer is working. It breaks encapsulation and it breaks self-organization. Actually, it breaks pretty much everything. Customers are not buying developer hours, they are buying software. Their focus needs to be on how much software they can expect in a given time period, and to adjust scope to meet dates or stay in budget.

Story points help set expectations here. Very soon after beginning iterative development using a size measure to estimate, customers will be able to see the capacity of the team, e.g. "This team can deliver 40 units of software per iteration, therefore let me prioritize 40 units' worth of features for the next iteration, with a few extra units in reserve." It is beautifully simple. A customer is welcome to map story points to cost (it will be approximate). He should not care about how many hours it took to make the software.

Argument #3: Story points will map to time anyway, and very soon we'll see that (e.g.) one story point is worth 2.5 hours, so it is better to skip the intermediate step and just measure in hours.

This is a flawed argument, and assumes a team never gets better. Truly self-organized teams always get better. When a new team starts, it may well be safe to say that one story point is worth 2.5 hours, but as the team improves its development and teamwork skills, as the code base is salvaged from the big mud hole it has been in for the past months or years and rises majestically to a state of elegance, and as the team uses regular reflection to improve its process, the value of a single story point will change. It may come to be valued at only two hours, because time is being used more effectively. Now instead of 40 story points in an iteration, the team can take on 50 story points.

More story points per sprint means that the customer will be getting more software. The cost of this software will not go down; the team building it will be making greater profits for the company. That's business. The customer is happy—happier, in fact—he is getting the software he needs at the price he expects to pay, but getting it faster. Everyone benefits.

Imagine the scenario where the customer measured development time. He would expect his software to get cheaper as the team got better; what used to take twenty hours to build now only takes ten hours, because the developers have put time into creating a good infrastructure and developing good practices. This does not seem right. The benefits of improvement should at the very least be shared equally between provider and customer. A time-based estimation model will not allow for that without (apparent) steep price increases.

A measure of size allows a team to show they are creating more value for money, assuming work has been prioritized for true business value (any estimate of effort is meaningless by itself, and is only one half of the ROI calculation required for intelligent business practice). We can draw velocity charts to show this. A measure of time will never reveal this, as there are always a fixed number of working hours in an iteration.

Argument 4: Story points don't allow you to improve your estimation techniques.

Actually, they do. Sometimes when clients ask me how this works, or why it works, I tell them it is magic. This is not so far from the truth. I have never really figured out quite why or how it works, but it does. Teams just get better at estimating. A simple velocity chart that maps two points for each iteration, specifically estimated points and actual points, will begin to show the lines converging over time, and not that much time either. Of course, the shorter the iterations, the quicker this improvement will become apparent. I usually recommend iteration lengths of one week or two weeks. It is rare that longer iterations add much value to the process.

And to be clear, the two lines don't just get closer together because teams are committing to less and less work each time. The average value of points delivered goes up over time. The latter, it may be argued, is because teams begin to game the system, making bigger and bigger estimates. I can see how that would be a temptation, but because the team starts collecting historical data, they self-correct for this, using their data as a baseline for future measurement. Remember, good software developers want to build good software, and they want to do it fast and efficiently. Suspicion and mistrust don't have much of a home in an agile environment.

May 21st, 2007

Estimation II: Time

The two favored measures of estimation in agile software development over the years have been ideal person hours (original scrum) and story points (XP, and later scrum). I think both fall short of being useful. The first, simply because software isn't built by individual persons, but by teams, and the second because it adds a level of indirection to the question customers really care about: How long will it take?

Joshua Kerievsky has written at length[1] about why he and his teams no longer use story points, and he describes their journey away from points. In the article he touches on team weeks:

> *I coach teams to write user stories for their releases and estimate them using "team weeks": the amount of time it will take the whole team to complete the work. It doesn't matter if only 2 people on a team of 10 can do the work: just provide the estimate as either .5, 1, 1.5 or 2 team weeks.*

In a healthy agile environment we have cross-functional teams, i.e. teams that have what is needed to take an idea from conception to working software. Rarely does one person have all the required skills, but a thoughtfully formed team of people will have the appropriate set of skills between them. So estimation can never be done in person days or hours. This will keep us in the divide-and-conquer mindset, and encourage hand-offs from one person to another. As Kerievsky points out, it doesn't matter if only two people on a larger team will do the work; the focus

[1] Joshua Kerievsky, "Stop Using Story Points," *Industrial Logic* (industriallogic.com), October 12, 2012

needs to be on team responsibility, hence team weeks—or, as is my preference, team days.

Very little has been written about this unit of measure, so I was glad to see it brought to light in Kerievsky's article. I have used this measure with teams on and off over the past few years and—if we are going to use estimation measures at all—I find this the most useful and meaningful measure. It seems to encourage realistic thinking, and generates engagement from team members during planning dialogs. Developers are actually very good at estimating, and using team-day estimation—a different take on "actual time"—creates a more engaged and respectful dialog between team members and customers.

While story points do encourage team-think, they sometimes fall short of being meaningful due to the high level of abstraction, which is easily abused. I once witnessed a team attempting to game the system in response to their manager pressuring for "increased velocity." Be careful what you ask for! There are only two weeks in a two-week sprint. There are only seven people on a seven-person team. Going faster can only mean going crappier.

Both scrum and kanban implementations can benefit from predictions of time-to-market. We know such predictions are never accurate, but for marketing and sales departments to do their job, we owe them our best guess. Team-day sizing can be quick and approximate, but gives enough of a sense of reality for a simple calculation to be done on release dates—using measures that mean the same thing to all parties.

October 17th, 2012

Estimation III: Don't Estimate

Most scrum teams these days are taught the estimation techniques described in Mike Cohn's *Agile Estimation and Planning*,[1] namely the estimating of user stories (aka requests) in relative size using story points, and the estimating of tasks in hours. I eschewed task estimates a few years ago, and more recently, perhaps over the past two to three years, I have found less and less need for story estimation. The practice is time-consuming, creates unnecessary overhead, and adds very little to a team's ability to make and meet commitments. On occasion the practice has caused irritation and distress in both team members and customers, who simply do not see any value in it.

I am in favor of teams and individuals experiencing short-term distress or even breakdown; this is often an important part of the learning process, but in the case of estimation I don't find it to be worthwhile. There are better things to focus on, such as writing well-formed user stories—requests that have clear value and conditions of acceptance. The dialog around defining the conditions of acceptance tends to cause requests to become smaller. It is very hard to create and agree on a set of acceptance criteria for large or vague requests.

If velocity is important (and I'm not convinced it is) then it can be figured through a count of completed requests. When requests are kept small, they tend to be much of the same size. If they are not, this may indicate a lack of clarity on two fronts:

[1] Mike Cohn, *Agile Estimation and Planning* (New Jersey: Prentice Hall, 2005)

what the customer or product owner is asking for, and what the team is committing to. Rather than slapping on a very large story point number. I think it is better to spend a little more time, think a little differently and refractor the request down into a set of smaller requests. I always recommend to teams that they take on between five and ten stories per sprint. Somehow this seems to work out no matter the domain or the length of sprint. Having smaller requests also aids the prioritization process as we learn what doesn't need to be done.

I have come to believe that estimation using any number system, whether it be ideal hours or relative points (which ultimately map to time) is compliance to an outmoded system, a way of appeasing old-school management who are unable, or perhaps more accurately unwilling, to think beyond data points and (empty) promises. There is still a mindset in the agile world, as much as there ever was in the world of project management, that teams can somehow commit to both time and scope. Estimation as it is commonly done perpetuates that myth, or at best does not challenge it.

A team is better served by committing on gut feeling rather than on data points. We are feeling people as much as we are thinking people; ironically the former may be more important when working in the knowledge industry. At the end of each planning meeting the team members should ask the question, "Do we honestly believe we can meet the commitment we just made?" If the answer is not a resounding "Yes!" then the team should reduce the commitment until it is. And no, this does not result in teams under-delivering. I have never once experienced that phenomenon. If your experience is different, perhaps you have other deeply rooted organizational dysfunction to deal with first.

Moving away from the obsession with numbers allows us to begin to trust our instincts, to draw on our individual real-world experiences and our "team intelligence" to give truthful responses to the "When will it all be done?" question.

If you find your team is bound by "estimation-think," I challenge you to spend a few sprints not estimating, but spending the time instead to make the stories in your backlog smaller, each having a clear value statement, and reasonable conditions of acceptance. You may be surprised by what happens.

January 24th, 2010

Scrum Roles: an Abstraction

Scrum was originally designed for software development but I have found it can be applied in many different business contexts, that is, if the underlying values and principles are understood. However, in attempting to describe scrum in a general way, I find I am dissatisfied by retaining the names of the scrum roles, as they seem too industry-specific or at least are loaded with meaning specific to current (often unsatisfactory) usage. In considering a fully industry-agnostic scrum, I'd like to attempt to recast these roles to their essence.

The Roles in Agnostic Scrum

1. The "What" Voice

A single voice, possibly channeling many voices, with the aim of defining "well-formed outcomes" and prioritizing for the highest possible value in the given context. The "what" voice is also responsible for expenditure and any go/no-go decision.

2. The "How" Tribe

A cross-functional group of three to seven people who between them contain all the skills necessary to solve the problems given by the voice. Only the members of the tribe are empowered to make decisions as to how to do the work, requesting clarity and support from the voice as necessary.

3. The Joker (or Jester)

An outcomes-neutral facilitator, concerned with fostering a collaborative environment, guiding the tribe towards self-improvement and self-sufficiency, and challenging the containing organization to lead through release and honor, rather than control and mistrust. The joker—the wild card in a deck of cards, independent, and unattached to any suit—acts as a servant to the team and an agent of change within the wider organization. The term joker in this context comes from Augusto Boal's *Theatre of the Oppressed.*[1]

Early feedback on the term "joker" has indicated it is a term not well suited to the corporate environment. I'm inclined to say, "hooray!" but I'm also open to better offers. David Koontz suggested the term "jester," in reference to the aphorism, "It is the jester that speaks truth to the king and lives to tell about it." Whatever name we choose, I believe it needs to reflect the agnostic, truth-telling, health-seeking spirit of the role, and should exclude the term "master."

These three roles constitute the scrum team; their tendency to pull in three different directions—profit, mastery and the greater good—is what generates the healthy conflict and tension required to reach previously unimagined levels of innovation and creativity, and allows scrum teams to deliver true value.

There is a fourth role in scrum, outside of the team, but involved at regular intervals. The role is essentially everyone else who cares.

4. The Audience

Everyone who funds, uses or profits from the product, service or idea being created. The audience offers feedback at regular intervals, and should contain among them a handful of serious

[1] Augusto Boal, *Theatre of the Oppressed*, (London: Pluto Press, 1979)

critics. The term "audience", in this context, was coined by Matt Heusser and Chris McMahon in an essay titled, "Performing the Software." [2]

The "What" is the destination; the "How" is the pathway

Calling the first role the "what" voice and the second role the "how" tribe instantly sets the two aspects of creation apart from one another. The What/How distinction separates the different acts of creation, *but it does not separate the players.* It is still vital for healthy dialog to take place between the requester and the responders. A request is not a demand, and needs to be open to counter-offers.

For self-organization to work a team (or tribe) needs to be empowered, left alone and trusted. Trusting is difficult when requirements are vague, and empowerment is impossible when the tribe experiences continuous interference regarding the technologies, tools and practices they are to use.

We need a clear separation between the value being requested and the path we'll take to produce that value. People on the business end of the creative process need to define desired outcomes that describe audience and value. And as they are likely not developing solutions themselves, they need to be completely feet-off the solution pathway, unless specifically invited to step in.

Looking at the scrum roles in this industry-agnostic way allows us to see the underlying principles by which the roles need to operate to be successful. It is too easy to get caught up in the day-to-day implementation decisions, and lose sight of the greater purpose.

October 8th, 2009

[2] Matt Heusser and Chris McMahon, "Performing the Software," *ST&P Magazine*, Volume 6, Issue 10, Oct 2009

Scrum Doesn't Do Anything

"Doing scrum" is as meaningless (and impossible) as creating an instance of an abstract class. Scrum is a framework for surfacing organizational dysfunction. It is not a process and it is not prescriptive. The core framework of scrum—as described in Ken Schwaber's books,[1, 2] on the Scrum Alliance website,[3] and in many other places—cannot actually do anything in and of itself. It is, in a sense, a contract we put in place between those seeking value and those building it. But a contract doesn't produce anything. An interface is passive. We need an implementation.

Scrum begins to work when people understand it well enough to create a concrete implementation, to emerge a process that is their own. Understanding and respecting the scrum framework and its set of guidelines allows you to become aligned with others—to have a common set of values and principles from which to operate.

Scrum itself can be thought of as similar to a set of game rules. Ken Schwaber is fond of using a chess analogy: the rules of chess are easy to learn, and knowing them means you can play the game with others, but as soon as you decide to change the rules, the whole game breaks down and you won't find an opponent to play with you. Chess is a competitive game, of course, and scrum is not, so I prefer to use a collaborative analogy, such as dance. A couples dance, like tango, requires that both parties dance

[1] Ken Schwaber and Mike Beedle, *Agile Software Development with Scrum*, (New Jersey: Prentice Hall, 2001)
[2] Ken Schwaber, *Agile Project Management with Scrum*, (Redmond, Washington: Microsoft Press, 2004)
[3] scrumalliance.org

by the same basic rules. There is a rhythm, there are steps, and there is posture. Once these basics are mastered, a couple can improvise within that framework. The rules of tango bind the couple together in a common pursuit of excellence. The added creativity takes the dance from a formulaic exercise into a thing of passion and beauty. In scrum you need to dance with others. It is the doing, not the knowing, that brings results. Scrum, like tango, requires people to develop relationships, to improvise, to take risks, to listen and to trust.

So respecting the contract, the rules, or in software parlance, respecting the interface, allows you to create a process that suits your context—and your context is many things... people, industry, business, market place, product, location, language, physical environment, culture, people. It starts and ends with people. Another way of looking at it might be to say that scrum doesn't actually do anything; people do things. The scrum process will emerge through the interaction of the workers, and it will be different for each organization or team. And this is where many trip up; they think that creating their own process starts with breaking the rules: it doesn't. Do that, and you have failed before you begin.

The scrum process an organization creates must operate within the agreed parameters, must be bounded by the rules. To use a software design analogy, all methods of the abstract class must be implemented, or the class won't compile: it won't work. Try to move your bishop in a straight line in a game of chess, and your opponent will leave the table. Pick up the soccer ball and throw it and you'll be red-carded.

The framework of scrum is a powerful mechanism for surfacing organizational and personal dysfunction. It is that very power that causes people to try to circumvent the rules, to take shortcuts. They don't want to look. But not looking doesn't cause problems to go away or broken things to mend, it just delays the inevitable big crash. We don't call out the value of courage in scrum for nothing.

Comparing scrum then to implementation practices such as XP or software craftsmanship makes little sense. Each of these movements offers excellent tools for implementing a solid scrum practice, for making the abstract concrete. Scrum offers a strong framework and a relentless rhythm to shake out the dust of years.

You cannot "do scrum" but you can certainly embrace it, and the more courageously you do, the stronger your emergent process will be.

October 11th, 2009

Marriage, But

The term "ScrumBut" [1] is popular these days, referring to an implementation of scrum that fails to embrace the whole framework ("Well, we are doing scrum, but..."). It is a common cause of the failure of scrum to take hold and actually be useful, and leaves scrum open to the criticism that it "doesn't work." Ways of working, or even ways of being, tend not to be effective when the frameworks designed to support the concepts are ignored, or given short shrift. This essay looks at another kind of framework: Marriage.

Marriage is a wonderful concept. It is a promise of love, togetherness, mutual nurturing and the creation of family. It exists in one form or another in all cultures, and it appeals to the majority of people in the world, each of us dreaming of a long-term mate, and the promise fulfilled.

And yet marriages fail—all the time. Why is this? Well, there are a myriad of reasons, but usually it comes down to the fact that the conditions—the rules if you like—for making marriage work are cast aside, or reformed to suit one or other of the individuals. If we listen closely to the language of a particular marriage we may hear subtext to the effect of... "Love is good and everything, but this honor thing doesn't quite work for me," "Until death, hm, that's an awfully long time," "Faithful really means just not telling," "I see the value of the 'in health' thing, but this 'in sickness' part isn't adding much to my personal happiness," "Can I rephrase that as 'for richer or not quite so rich'?

[1] Ken Schwaber, "ScrumBut," *Scrum.org* (scrum.org/ScrumBut)

If you're going to humiliate me by being poor you're on your own." And so on.

MarriageBut. It is the root cause of marriage failure: The inability or refusal to honor the contract. The contract is a very simple one, and there are many variations on the vows, so we are not asked to say things we don't believe in. We agree to live according to the framework, but so often when it starts to get difficult one or both partners start shifting the rules to suit themselves, undermining the foundation and ultimately causing the structure to fall apart. With a failed marriage myself, I say this with no judgment, only from a perspective of painful reflection.

The pertinent question for this essay is this: Does marriage fail? I'd argue strongly that "marriage" does not. Marriage as a framework, as a promise, is strong and robust. It has served humankind well for hundreds of centuries. There are tweaks and incremental improvements we can (in fact do) make, e.g. the removal of the words "to obey" from the woman's script in many modern Christian ceremonies, but for the most part the framework has been strong for a long time.

It is the instances of marriage that fail, the individual implementations. Few, after a failed marriage, would say that the concept itself is wrong. They may apportion blame to one another, or to outside forces (e.g. in-laws), but in the end they move on and often try a new implementation, learning from their previous experiences.

Marriage doesn't fail. Some marriages do. It is important to separate the model from the implementations, in this, and other aspects of our lives. If I build a house for myself using shoddy materials and poor techniques, is the concept of "home" a bad one? When a government is run by disingenuous, dishonest individuals does it make the concept of democracy a failure? I think most would agree that the failure is in the implementation rather than the idea.

Many are quick to knock the concept of self-organized business as a fad, or the scrum framework as too rigid, and point to a few failed implementations to discredit the concepts. But in essence the scrum concepts are good ones. They speak to the natural rhythms of our lives, and our very human need to collaborate and trust. Scrum, like marriage, is a contract, rooted in sound values. Each is a promise of an improved quality of life. Yes, we'll screw both up time after time: but still the ideas are strong.

May 3rd, 2011

Don't Have Meetings

While teaching an introductory scrum workshop, I came to the sudden realization that I didn't want to use the word "meeting" when talking about scrum. Meetings have such a bad rap in our industry, and rightly so. I recall hours-long, painful meetings where nothing moved forward, the louder people postured and argued, talked in circles and dug themselves into ever-deepening trenches, while the quieter ones stared sheepishly at the table, wishing they could be back in their cubicle doing useful work.

Admittedly, scrum has reduced this meeting overhead to a few key, timeboxed events but the legacy of "meeting culture" still hangs over us, heavily. "Scrum has too many meetings" is a common complaint... and then we discover that the complainant's daily meetings drag on for 40 minutes, that their retrospectives are unproductive, lack meaning or devolve into complaint sessions, while planning meetings are controlled and directive, leaving team members sullen and brow-beaten.

So the thought occurred to me, in the moment, that telling the workshop participants "these scrum meetings are essential" was likely to deflate them rather than excite them about this new way of working. Meeting culture has penetrated scrum, as it must. Something so heavy and oppressive, so entrenched in our way of being will crush anything that tries to challenge its power. The Scrum Alliance introduced the term "ceremony" to replace the term meeting, but that's almost as bad, and to some people even worse, carrying with it images of cults and cloaked figures preforming strange rituals. And using that term in the same sentence with "scrum master"... forget it!

So I used the term conversation. Scrum is centered on people, and people have conversations. There are conversations to plan, conversations to align, and conversations to reflect. We have these conversations at the appropriate times, and for the appropriate durations in order to inform our work. If we don't have these conversations, we won't know what we are doing (planning), we won't know where we are going (alignment), and we'll keep repeating the same mistakes (reflection). Expressed this way, I felt a lifting of interest in the room, a lightening of hearts. I had essentially told this group of people "you never have to be in a meaningless meeting again." And I believe that.

Let's stop talking about meetings. In fact, let's stop having meetings. Little of value comes out of a traditional business meeting. People in collaborative dialog though, now that's exciting—that's meaningful.

March 25th, 2011

Timebox != Commitment

Procrastinating one evening, I got lost in a long stream of tweets about timeboxing, fascinated at how much disdain was aimed at a simple unit of time, and how it was blamed for sloppy workmanship, poor quality, panic and many other dysfunctional behaviors.

Having already given up on doing anything I needed to do that night, I jumped into the stream to challenge this point of view. After a few back and forth exchanges I realized the disdain arose not from anything a timebox actually is, but what people confuse it with.

It seems there is an understanding of a timebox that goes something like this:

1. Set a timebox size.
2. Commit to a bunch of work.
3. Realize you are failing to complete it all.
4. Rush to finish.
5. Produce crappy work.
6. Be exhausted.
7. Go to #2—repeat until dead, or company goes out of business.

The only part of this that has anything to do with timeboxing is #1. The rest is about making promises you can't keep, and doing it again and again. Timebox antagonists call this commitment.

Here's my understanding of timeboxing:

1. Set a timebox size.
2. Engage in dialog with requester/s. Review and prepare requests. Prioritize.
3. Select a request, small enough to fit inside the timebox.
4. Complete the work to the satisfaction of the requester.
5. Breathe [reassess remaining requests if necessary].
6. Go to #3—until there is no request that can fit in the remaining time.
7. Stop work [if time remaining, take slack[1] time].
8. Reflect. Learn from mistakes, and adapt accordingly.
9. Go to #2—repeat until all requests met, or deadline reached.

Hard to really get the essence of this in pseudo-code, but I think it's reasonably clear. There is still commitment in this approach, but it is a reasonable, wise commitment. The work committed to is independent of the timebox length. The timebox is there to create rhythm, and to create space. It is a heartbeat; that is all.

Life abounds with natural rhythms; finding our own work rhythm and honoring it is a beautiful thing. It requires release though—an alignment with life.

If you are using a timebox to force commitment in order to meet externally imposed goals, and you are not changing your behavior when this becomes apparent, then perhaps your focus is in the wrong place. You can continue to blame the timebox, shedding responsibility, or you can exert courage and look inward, towards self.

April 20th, 2012

[1] I use the term "slack" here as defined in Tom DeMarco's book *Slack: Getting Past Burnout, Busywork, and the Myth of Total Efficiency* (New York: Crown Business, 2002)

The Retrospective is Now

In her 1958 book *The Art of Making Dances* [1] the dancer and choreographer Doris Humphrey offered the following advice: "Never leave the ending until the end." Since first hearing that advice in the late 1970s I have found it to be appropriate in all creative endeavors I have undertaken. It essentially asks that we have a sense of the whole before filling in the detail. It is a very agile concept. If she had been addressing a business audience, Ms. Humphrey may have recommended that we know why we are doing something before we undertake the doing of it—that we have a clear vision. In other words, we need to ask ourselves: what value are we seeking... what story are we telling?

Traditional software development tended to leave the ending to the end, which is why we often joke about teams being ninety percent done ninety percent of the time, and why everything goes pear-shaped when we try to integrate all the disparate pieces.

Taking Doris Humphrey's original insight, we can apply it to a different aspect of agile software development: the retrospective. Reframed, the statement might read: never leave the retrospecting until the retrospective.

Many agilists promote something known as the "retrospective prime directive," originally penned by Norm Kerth: [2]

> *Regardless of what we discover, we understand and truly believe that everyone did the best job he or she could, given what was*

[1] Doris Humphrey, *The Art of Making Dances* (New York: Grove Press, 1959)
[2] Norman L. Kerth, *Project Retrospectives: A Handbook for Team Reviews*, (New York: Dorset House, 2001)

known at the time, his or her skills and abilities, the resources available, and the situation at hand.

I personally find this so-called "directive" somewhat condescending and superficial, and believe its use does not foster the kind of environment that allows real, meaningful change to occur. The retrospective prime directive was written at a time when retrospectives were more commonly known as "postmortems," and would occur at the end of a (sometimes very long) project. In such situations tempers were worn, and the propensity to blame was rife. Having people believe, or at least act as if they believed, that everyone had done their best was a way to reduce the heat of such a meeting—which was named postmortem for a reason!

In an agile context we value frequent inspection. Introduction of the prime directive into an agile retrospective seems to assume no reflection has been done on the journey to the retrospective, that all feedback, criticism, concern, all differences and disputes are bottled up and saved for a single meeting at the end of a sprint. If that is the way a team is taught to work, then I can see the need for such a directive. But imposing a belief of "bestness" after the fact parallels the traditional approach to testing, where QA specialists try to test quality into a piece of software after it has been built. Both approaches are sub-optimal, and wasteful.

On the other hand, if a team is given the opportunity to reflect each day a new mood is generated. The team members self-organize toward a collaborative and trusting way of being, learning to confront the tough moments with courage and respect. We then see the quality of interaction and collaboration woven into the fabric of the team, not patched on at some later date. We might call this reflection-driven development. With such teams the retrospective requires no directives, admonishments or rules of conduct.

In fact, without the necessity to take the lid off Pandora's box every two or three weeks, the retrospective becomes something much more interesting and powerful. It becomes a moment of stillness and reflection, a time to breathe out, to say thank you. A time to be, and not do. Such a retrospective results in the team members feeling closer to one another as human beings. It is a deepening of the tribal spirit, the common consciousness, that intangible element inherent in all groups striving for a common purpose.

Seek small adjustments as and when needed, and you won't have to worry about the big changes: They will take care of themselves. And maybe you will experience a shifting of self, from which place the real organizational change will emerge.

If teams struggle with the ongoing feedback model—and new teams often do, I'd like to offer a different way to begin a retrospective, i.e. to enter the sharing, reflective mindset required for this conversation. It is not a directive, not a statement to publicly proclaim, but simply something for each team member to quietly consider before dialog begins—and the wording here is suggestive only, not a script to be followed:

We are emotional and vulnerable beings, subject to a continuous flow of influences from a myriad of sources. Sometimes we perform magnificently; other times we mess up. Mostly we are somewhere between these extremes. In this last period of work everyone did what they did, and likely had reasons for doing so. Accept what is. And now, what can we learn from our past actions and thinking that will inform and guide our future ones?

Foster the reflective mindset, and retrospecting will occur throughout your journey, allowing your end-of-sprint meeting to take on a new quality altogether, perhaps one of love and celebration.

January 22nd, 2011

The Soul of Scrum

Scrum was designed and refined for small teams working in a co-located space, willing to innovate and able to get working software out of the door in a rapid fashion. It is simple, elegant and has a proven track record in such environments. Sadly, too many captains of industry believe it is a cure-all for any software environment, and attempt to employ it without adaption in large, cumbersome organizations deeply infected with a command-and-control mindset, within companies where teams are distributed across cities and countries, and in non-software environments. This is like trying to hammer a square peg into a round hole. I believe force-fitting scrum causes more devastation than repair.

This is not to say that the underlying principles of scrum do not have a wide applicability; They do. The problem is that too many scrum enthusiasts don't actually understand what these principles are, or why they are important. Many managers, consultants, coaches and scrum masters focus on systems, processes, and practices—and worse, attempt to incorporate "scrum" into their existing, very un-scrum patterns of work, creating some weird, freakish chimera, fit for no purpose.

Using scrum as a band-aid will fail. Always. Evidence shows that it has, time and time again. Compliance to brand names or prescribed systems always causes this kind of damage. People stop thinking for themselves, stop innovating and then get frustrated, indignant and resistant when things don't go according to plan. Scrum is the new compliance. That is its tragedy.

Rather than trying to use scrum as a magic bullet, I recommend treating it as an abstract class, a platonic ideal. Contained in an effective implementation of scrum there exists a set of principles, which when abstracted out can be applied in a plethora of situations to create environments that foster engagement, creativity and true value. This is how I understand the soul of scrum, and how I describe its inherent principles:

Scrum Principles

1. Focus

The primary principle. When creating scrum at Easel Corp in 1993,[1] Jeff Sutherland saw the dysfunction many of us see today. He identified it as a culture of scarcity: never enough time, people, resources, or money. Many things were being treated as high priority, with the result that nothing was prioritized. Sutherland figured that if the team could do one thing at a time, then that one thing (product, project, feature) would have all the time, people, etc. that it required. It could be done to completion, thus freeing up the minds of the team members up to fully focus on the most important thing. Using the principle of focus, the organization moved from a culture of scarcity to a culture of abundance. Focusing on one thing at a time is a simple idea—indeed, an obvious one—and it works.

2. Alignment

In order to meet business and user needs, development teams need to engage with their stakeholders frequently. Most of our pain in software development comes from misalignment. Requirements are misunderstood, or poorly transmitted; what customers and users think they want is often not what they actually need; assumptions are made about levels of understanding; and long development cycles mean mistakes don't surface

[1] Jeff Sutherland, "Agile Development: Lessons Learned From The First Scrum," (scrumalliance.org/resources/35), October, 2004

until the cost of adjustment has become untenable. Well-aligned teams meet frequently with stakeholders, to plan at the start of each iteration, reflect at the end, and when appropriate check in during a development cycle. Alignment conversations need to be wholly collaborative, with each participant or participating group respecting the knowledge and experience of the others.

3. Artful Making

This term was introduced to the software world by Lee Devin and Rob Austin in the book *Artful Making.*[2] Devin, a theatre director, and Austin, a business professor, proposed that for any team to be successful in a creative and improvisational space (which is exactly what software development is, at its heart) four qualities are required. They name these as: release, collaboration, ensemble, and play. This suggests the idea that a team needs to be given freedom for its members to interact, so that a collaborative environment is fostered, leading to ensemble, where both the thing being created and the team itself are larger and more interesting than any one person's input: the whole is greater than the sum of its parts. For this to happen, a spirit of play needs to be encouraged, risks need to be taken, failure embraced as a learning opportunity—and team members learn to take the product or business goals seriously, rather than themselves!

4. Self-organization

Groups of humans are, by nature, complex adaptive systems, and thus self-organizing. We attempt to impose control and direction on individuals through management techniques such as work assignment, status reporting, daily or weekly progress reports and other mechanisms that usually only serve to waste time and produce compliant—or irritated, rebellious—individuals.

[2] Rob Austin and Lee Devin, *Artful Making: What Managers Need to Know About How Artists Work*, (New Jersey: Financial Times Prentice Hall, 2003)

Self-organization relies on the simple idea that the people closest to the problem are the best people to solve the problem. In software this means developers are the best people to figure out how to write software, given good dialog around the requirements and acceptance criteria. Self-organization is not anarchy. It is not chaos. It is freedom to innovate. It requires the involvement of all parties: customers, management and workers alike. Between them they set clear goals and boundaries which allow teams to develop solutions suited to a purpose, using the best tools they have access to. Self-organization begins with release, and is fostered through the other three qualities of artful making.

5. Rhythm

Without time boundaries and regular alignment conversations, all of the above becomes wishy-washy and flimsy. Rhythm is the framework that holds all of this together, and allows organizations to move quickly (without rushing and panicking) and to uncover mistakes and errors of judgment within hours or days, rather than weeks or months… or worst case, at the end! Scrum introduces the idea of a timebox, where an agreement is made at the start, and where the work, product, and process are reflected upon at the end. Scrum timeboxes tend to be between one and three weeks long. All product alignment conversations should have regular days/times, so everyone can clear their calendars ahead of time and be prepared in advance. Team members should also meet daily for internal alignment. Having a regular heartbeat for a sprint also allows some downtime between each one; time to breathe, to think, to explore new ideas. Rhythm ultimately leads to flow. The idea that working continuously will provide instant flow is misguided. It will lead to a pile up.

The scrum framework itself relies on these five principles: Alignment plus rhythm gives us the empirical process; rhythm gives us timeboxing and regular check-ins; focus helps manage a backlog, and, coupled with alignment, makes for wise sprint commitments; artful making and self-organization create the environment for teams to produce excellent solutions to business problems. Using these principles mindfully will help any organization, large or small, local or distributed, software or otherwise create a way of working that is fully aligned with scrum, and yet isn't scrum.

The scrum framework is a skeleton, and we flesh it out with process and practices. This is good, providing we are always context-sensitive. Yet without its soul, scrum will always be an automaton, always controlled by, and at the mercy of, outside forces. It will never be truly emergent—and free.

February 15th, 2012

Culture

The Promised Land

To thrive in the business world today we need the speed of the human mind, racing ahead of our stumbling footfalls; we need the immediacy of eye contact and physical touch (embrace me, fellow traveler), and we need the creativity of the collaborative spirit, unleashed through trust and self-organization, eyes filled with wonderment, nerves tingling. Maybe then we stand a chance.

Catastrophic Organizational Change

I find something important to be explored in the term "catastrophic organizational change," a phrase coined by Michael Ivey to describe the paradigm shift necessary for an organization to embrace agility. [1] Many balked at this phrase, responding in a somewhat reactionary, and even fearful way.

Catastrophic organizational change is an interesting and rich term, one with a powerful, anarchic edge, but at the same time tinged with compassion. New paradigms need new language, so I am not put off by the negative connotations of the word catastrophe. Until Jeff Sutherland adopted the term to describe a software development process, the word "scrum" itself belonged to the sport of rugby and meant "a disordered or confused situation involving a number of people." [2] Language can change to meet the need of the speakers, to meet the need of the cause. It is adaptive—and happily so.

Catastrophic organizational change is a new phrase, but not a new concept. Catastrophic change comes about when people discover their own truth, by pushing their own and others' comfort zones to the limit, by taking risks, embracing failure and walking through fear. That's real change. That's breakthrough. I don't believe placing a methodology like scrum, or XP, or any of the other brand-name agile methodologies onto a broken organization really, truly solves anything. It is yet another band-aid.

[1] Michael D. Ivey, ScrumDevelopment Yahoo! Group, November 19, 2005

[2] *The American Heritage® Dictionary of the English Language, Fourth Edition* (New York: Houghton Mifflin Company, 2000)

A better one than most, there's little doubt, but a wide chasm still exists between the presenting problem and the sickness that still lingers below the surface—and feeds.

I heard Jon Spence make a very poignant comment at the 2005 Scrum Gathering: "Success is our enemy." It is the small, short-term successes that are so dangerous—those that will have us believe we are making real progress, when in fact we are only putting a new coat of paint over a crumbling facade. Such a superficial approach is not sustainable. Can scrum, in and of itself, be successful? I doubt it. Well, define "success." Come to that, define "scrum"!

Writing great software and delivering high customer value on time is a noble goal to be sure, but self-actualization, artistry... that's where I want to go. How does this agile paradigm shift fit into... well, everything? How can we shift the balance of power, not just from one person/group to another, but shift in the sense of redistribution? How can we completely undermine the status quo and introduce new ways of doing things that none of us have even thought of yet? Can we? Should we? Big questions, but surely worth asking from time to time.

There are many top-down and heavy-handed approaches to organizational change that will result in catastrophe. But they will not result in meaningful change, and that is the point that the critics of catastrophic organizational change seem to be missing. The focus is on change—deep change, real change. The focus is not on catastrophe. Catastrophe is the journey, not the destination. The weapons of catastrophic change are not sledge hammers and bulldozers; rather they are craftsman's tools, delicate and accurate, operated with patience and love.

Fundamental change does not happen from the top-down. There is too much at stake for the participants, too much to lose when things don't go as planned. Change happens from within (ask any psychotherapist) and in the context of an organization, that means bottom-up. Forget executive advocates; get junior programmer advocates, get admin assistants, get those with no power. Seed the lowest level of the organization with agents of passion: educate them, nurture them, make knowledge available, have conversations, share stories, laugh, agitate and ask difficult questions. Be unafraid. Change will be much slower, but it will be real and yes, it may well be catastrophic.

The 1904 San Francisco earthquake did not happen overnight. It took years of tiny, subtle shifts in the underlying rock strata before the foundations of the city just collapsed: catastrophic change. The French Revolution did not just occur on a whim. Small groups of people were changing their own hearts and minds, and those of others around them, until the force grew so big it finally exploded: catastrophic change. Termites eat buildings from the inside. The destruction remains invisible until it is too late to do anything about it: catastrophic change. In all these cases we can mourn the catastrophe, or we can embrace the change.

Catastrophic change starts with the individual (or more specifically, the individual in the context of his group, within the organization, and within the larger society in which he exists). I don't know exactly what the focus needs to be to initiate that change, but I plan to explore the possibilities, and learn. One thing I do know: It needs to reach beyond the world of technology and science and into the world of art.

Today, among other activities, I have a part-time consulting contract with a software product company in Silicon Valley where the focus is on introducing iterative, incremental development. No talk of catastrophe, I just show up and do the next right thing. But even with the small goals, it is important for me to be genuine and speak my truth. Agility is not a set of practices; it is a way of being. I firmly believe that, and I trust it.

December 5, 2005

Agile Anarchy

Anarchy is a term most of us in the corporate world eschew. It has no place, we think, in a world of discipline, control, and bottom lines. And yet more and more corporations are embracing agile. Interesting conflict.

Agile is a compassionate form of anarchy—a gentle movement away from hierarchical, controlling structures toward collaborative, self-organized ones. The compassionate anarchist values his fellow humans on an equal footing, encourages emergent solutions, supports individual empowerment, and seeks to avoid dehumanization and marginalization. The parallels with agile are clear. Both the anarchist and the agilist believe that real change does not come about through compliance and coercion, cannot be commanded from on high, but begins at a grassroots level, with the individual. Each one of us is responsible for change. That is our beginning.

I have hand-picked a few quotes that suitably describe this view of anarchy.

> *Anarchism, to me, means not only the denial of authority, not only a new economy, but a revision of the principles of morality. It means the development of the individual as well as the assertion of the individual. It means self-responsibility, and not leader worship.*
>
> —*Voltairine de Cleyre* [1]

[1] Voltairine de Cleyre *Selected works of Voltairine de Cleyre*, (New York : Mother earth Pub. Association, 1914),

People forgot that industry is not an end in itself, but should be only a means to insure to man his material subsistence and to make accessible to him the blessings of a higher intellectual culture. Where industry is everything and man is nothing begins the realm of a ruthless economic despotism whose workings are no less disastrous than those of any political despotism.

—Rudolf Rocker[2]

Anarchism is a philosophy of freedom. It is a body of revolutionary ideas which reconciles, as no other revolutionary concept does, the necessity for individual freedom with the demands of society. It is a philosophy which starts from the individual and works upwards, instead of starting from the State and working downwards. Social structure in an anarchist society would be carefully and consciously kept to a minimum and would be strictly functional; where organization is necessary, it would be maintained, but there would be no organization for its own sake. This would help to prevent the hardening of organizations into institutions – the hard core of government.

—Bill Christopher, Jack Robinson,
Philip Sansom and Peter Turner[3]

Compassion is what keeps anarchy from degenerating into violent chaos and individual autonomy from resulting in disrespect and disregard for others. Anarchy is what keeps our compassion from becoming a hollow shell of the real thing—it's what keeps our love for others from becoming a commodity that is sold back to us or a ploy to make us acquiescent to the dictates of authority. Compassionate anarchy is about finding and

[2] Rudolf Rocker, Anarcho-Syndicalism (London: Pluto Press, 1989)
[3] Bill Christopher, Jack Robinson, Philip Sansom and Peter Turner. "The Relevance of Anarchism," in *The State Is Your Enemy: Selections From Freedom 1965-86* (London: Freedom Press, 1991)

> *appreciating the genuine soul in human beings and keeping it free from all authority, submission, moralism, and static roles.*
>
> —*anarchopedia.org*

> *I am an anarchist not because I believe anarchism is the final goal, but because there is no such thing as a final goal.*
>
> —*Rudolf Rocker*[4]

There are many good ideas, lurking in the dark recesses of the counter-culture. One of the great things that agile offers the corporate world is the freedom to seek outside the confines of what is considered right and proper, to embrace ideas that only a decade ago would have been considered anathema to corporate entities. Courage is touted as a key agile value by some agile pioneers, and it is certainly required when we reach out beyond our safety zone and listen to good ideas hitherto considered despicable, or dangerous. In the long run, the only safe (and sane) course is to go ahead and take the occasional risk.

June 10, 2009

[4]Rudolf Rocker, *The London Years* (London: Robert Anscombe & Co. Ltd, 1956)

Riding a Dinosaur

This essay was written in response to the news that the CEO of the Project Management Institute (PMI) had been invited to give a keynote talk at a Scrum Alliance gathering, an organization I once belonged to, worked for, and believed represented the future of scrum. That I no longer affiliate with the Scrum Alliance in no way conflicts with the sentiment expressed in this essay.

The Project Management Institute (PMI) is a large, powerful organization that has long promoted Tayloresque management principles.[1] Many people respect, even revere the organization, but I see it as an oppressor. Let me put this in context. The Orlando Scrum Gathering is approaching, and Gregory Balestrero, the Chief Executive Officer of the PMI has been invited, with much fanfare, to be one of the keynote speakers at the event. I object to this. Not because I have anything against the man (I'd never heard of him until now) but because I feel uncomfortable with the idea that the Scrum Alliance is turning to the PMI to learn... what? I don't know. After three years of seeking to understand I haven't yet found a good reason to listen to the voice of the PMI. This is tough to say as I know it upsets a lot of people in the scrum community.

Inviting someone to do a keynote speech implies they have something important to say—something that we need to hear. Balestrero, the man, may have something important to say, but

[1] Frederick Winslow Taylor, *The Principles of Scientific Management* (New York, London: Harper & Brothers, 1911)

Balestrero the CEO of the PMI does not. The PMI is an outmoded organization which represents and promotes, a particular way of working now known to be largely flawed in the context of software development. That the PMI wants to change itself is good news. That the PMI has an important message for scrum practitioners is unlikely.

If Mr. Balestrero is interested in learning about scrum, then have him attend the Scrum Gathering as a participant. I welcome him there, as I welcome anyone who wants to learn about scrum. I have no reason to believe Mr. Balestrero is anything other than a genuine man, with a desire to learn new things. No doubt he is also a very smart and passionate man to be where he is today. Such drive and passion are always welcome in the scrum world. I would just rather have him attend the gathering simply as Gregory, not as "the chief ambassador for advancing the profession of project management on behalf of PMI," as the Scrum Alliance's publicity material described him. I have no interest in hearing "powerful messages about the importance of project management in achieving success in today's global business environment." The corporate rhetoric is tiresome, and I don't buy it.

Scrum, as I understand it—as I live it—has nothing to do with project management. Personally I eschew the term "agile project manager" and consider it an oxymoron. Ken Schwaber has often made the statement that there is no project manager role in scrum. Indeed there is not, so why partner with the Project Management Institute? It starts to feel like compliance to the existing status quo, and appeasement to what is still a very powerful organization, albeit one whose power is threatened. It makes me wary.

I have always seen the move to agile as a software revolution, throwing off the weight of oppression and releasing us into a new way of being. The tragedy of many revolutions is that once successful, the leaders tend towards the same behavior that caused the need for the revolution in the first place. The oppressed become the oppressors, i.e. they take on essentially the same behaviors because they don't know how else to behave.[2]

George Orwell characterized this tendency in the novel *Animal Farm*, an allegory for the Russian Revolution and subsequent events. By the end of the book, the revolutionary leader, Napoleon—a pig—is walking on two legs, dressing in human clothing and selling his best friends out for horse meat.[3]

Why does the Scrum Alliance want to work with the PMI—a dinosaur in this ever-evolving, fast-changing agile world? It is surely a step backwards. Let me be clear: I see absolute value in working with those individual members of the PMI who care about scrum, but I see no value in working with the organization. It has some influence today, but that influence is waning in the light of agile—it was never particularly useful to the software industry in the first place. I say leave it be, let it die. Let's all seek entirely new ways of collaborating and advancing our professional skills. Giant monolithic institutions representing "the interests" of their members may not be the way of the 21st century. Maybe small is better. I sincerely hope that the Scrum Alliance won't scale to PMI proportions. (To date, this hope has not been fulfilled. At the time of publication the Scrum Alliance had over a quarter of a million active members, a largely unelected board of directors, and a total of seven certification programs.) Instead I'd like to see it splinter into small passionate self-managing groups, each with a slightly different agenda and different interests.

I perceive oppression not only from the PMI, but from corporate monoliths in general; they are by definition incredibly heavy and immovable. I am uncomfortable with the burgeoning relationship between the PMI and the scrum community, thinking

[2] Paulo Freire, *The Pedagogy of the Oppressed (Pedagogia do Oprimido)*, translated by Myra Bergman Ramos (New York: Herder and Herder, 1970)
[3] George Orwell, *Animal Farm* (New York, Harcourt, Brace, 1954)

I'd rather have us stay focused on our goal of transformation, stay true to our cause, and not be derailed by delusions of grandiosity. Four legs good. Period.

March 11th, 2009

Corporate Oppression

Oppression: The unjustifiable placing of a burden on someone or some group, by interfering with their powers, interests, or opportunities. Oppression may be deliberate, or an unintended outcome of social arrangements; it may be recognized for what it is, or may go unremarked even by those oppressed.

– *The Oxford Dictionary of Philosophy*[1]

We tend to think of oppression only in its deliberate form, when used as a weapon to subdue the conquered or to quell the sense of unrest and the spirit of uprising in the lower classes; but oppression exists in many forms and does not only affect poor, underprivileged people. We can observe many levels of oppression in large organizations today among middle class, well paid professionals.

As an example, consider cubicle culture, so ingrained in our idea of how people work in the software industry—yes still, even after 10+ years of agile. Isolating someone in a cubicle is an act of control, a way of ensuring compliance. Prisons throughout the world use the concept of solitary confinement as a form of punishment—some would say punishment bordering on the cruel and unusual: it is that deeply unnatural for people to be isolated from one another. One's imagination does not have to be stretched far to see the similarities between a corporate cubicle and a one-man prison cell. Without the support of their fellows, an individual is more vulnerable to suggestion and more

[1] Simon Blackburn, *The Oxford Dictionary of Philosophy*, (Oxford, New York: Oxford University Press, 1994)

likely to toe the line. Is this the deliberate intention of a cube farm? Possibly not, but it is the outcome.

But oppression goes far beyond office layouts. Games of power are played out daily—often with great zest within the upper echelons, but with ever-dwindling willingness as we move down towards the grassroots of an organization. The oppression that takes place is sometimes conscious, but more often is "an unintended outcome of social arrangements," and manifests itself in the oft-heard phrase, "It's just the way we do things around here."

Such oppression is usually hidden beneath the niceties of corporate behavior, beneath so-called socially acceptable norms. At its most insidious it hides beneath a facade of "fun," "teamwork," "community spirit" and other such fashionable buzzwords. In the oppressed people it takes the form of silent compliance, the fear of making mistakes, and a general sense that it is better to make no decision than to make the wrong one. It is better to delay than to act. The result of this corporate oppression is inertia: It is stagnation. If this oppression is not recognized for what it is, it cannot possibly be surfaced and dealt with. An organization groaning under the burden of such oppression can never be agile, no matter how many nice facades it puts on itself.

In addition to oppression at the individual company level, we often find a fear-based culture within companies, a culture of compliance to "standards," e.g. SOX, ISO 9001, CMMi. I have twice observed the effort exerted to meet such standards by those forced to comply, and both times it was a pathetic sight—fearful workers, terrified of making mistakes, outwardly exhausted and inwardly cowering. I don't exaggerate. Others may have a different experience; this was mine.

But who is responsible for the way things are? The oppressors? Society? It would be easy to apportion blame, and carry on the same way. The reality is that the oppressed person himself is the culprit. In a democratic society we have choices. If we are oppressed (and we are) it is because we choose to live that way.

There can be no really pervasive system of oppression...without the consent of the oppressed.

— Florynce Kennedy[2]

This is all well and good, and a simple two-step solution would be to a) recognize it, and b) act differently. The reality is trickier. Too often the oppressed don't want change; they simply want to be on the other side of the oppression. That is the ugly reality we live in. We have all seen individuals rise to middle-management and change behavior accordingly, fitting in to the system and emulating their superiors. Many of us have seen teams fall apart through in-fighting—indeed a key part of any good scrum master training course is focused on dealing with such situations. Reward systems in most software corporations are based on individual superiority, and to be superior, others must be considered inferior.

Commenting on the syndrome of in-fighting between oppressed natives in colonized countries, the Brazilian philosopher and education theorist Paulo Freire notes "Because the oppressor exists within their oppressed comrades, when they attack those comrades they are indirectly attacking their oppressor as well."[3]

He goes on to say, "On the other hand, at a certain point in their existential experience the oppressed feel an irresistible attraction towards the oppressors and their way of life. Sharing this way of life becomes an overpowering aspiration. In their alienation, the oppressed want at any cost to resemble the oppressors, to imitate them, to follow them."

If large monolithic bodies such as the IEEE and PMI are the

[2] Florynce Kennedy (1916-2000) was the first black woman to graduate from Columbia Law School. She was a social activist, feminist, co-founder of the National Organization for Women, and founder of the National Black Feminist Organization.
[3] Paulo Freire, *The Pedagogy of the Oppressed (Pedagogia do Oprimido)*, translated by Myra Bergman Ramos (New York: Herder and Herder, 1970)

oppressors in the software industry, then it follows from Freire's observations that the smaller process innovators, the ones who once kicked back against the style of management represented by these bodies, will now wish to emulate them, to essentially become them. The Scrum Alliance events, for example, are moving from intimate gatherings of passionate people to corporate-sponsored events with big-name keynote speakers, in essence becoming identical to all the other mainstream software conferences. The PMI, champions of the oft-scorned waterfall process, are now being looked to for advice and support (See the earlier essay in this collection, "Riding a Dinosaur"). This isn't progress, it is regression, or at best circularity. The spirit of revolution so apparent in the beginning of this movement has all but disintegrated, as we march to the corporate drum.

Where does scrum fit into a landscape of compliance and corporate emulation? Quite possibly it will be absorbed back into that culture, watered down, commoditized. It will be made nice. And in a few decades' time a new generation of dissatisfied, disempowered workers will start the revolution all over again.

We all desire change, but evidence indicates we don't know how to go about getting it in any deep and lasting way. By recognizing the reality of the oppression we live in, by facing it, acknowledging its truth, perhaps we can shake off the shackles of ingrained behaviors and begin to think and behave in new ways. And in doing so perhaps we can reinvent the world—or for now, at least the software industry.

March 16th, 2009

Organizational Blobs

Following the initial publication of my "catastrophic organizational change" essay I received some thoughtful feedback from Mishkin Berteig, who countered my position, arguing that, "Catastrophic change at any level is the sign of disease. As agile coaches, trainers, practitioners, we should be encouraging a healthy cycle of crisis and victory not a process of crisis, crisis, crisis, CRISIS, CATASTROPHE, change." [1] So I thought it useful to extend my thoughts on this topic.

When we talk about change, it's important to be specific. Everything changes all the time, whether we want it to or not. Change in an organizational context is really about improvement.

I concur that improvement, rather than being all-at-once, needs to be continual.[2] The small crises that trigger the changes that help us improve are learning opportunities—if recognized and responded to sooner rather than later. They inform us, we learn, we adapt, we improve.

I'm not saying that change *must* be catastrophic; I am observing that it often is, and that if we try to avoid that kind of change, or run from it, we end up with no change at all, or perhaps even more damaging (in its untruth), "pretend change" or "surface change."

There are different levels of change within an organization,

[1] Personal correspondence.

[2] I see a difference between continuous and continual improvement. The former implies that every change is an improvement, and that improvement is always occurring. This is rarely true. Some changes take us backwards, some will even cause failure. But over time we want to see a trend of improvement, thus I prefer the term continual, which allows for the inevitable setback without it being a cause for concern.

including team change and personal change. Berteig is right in this sense: catastrophic change at a team level is not necessary, and not desirable. Teams—certainly scrum teams—work with leaders, or coaches, or are fully self-organized; in all cases they work within a clear and solid inspect/adapt framework which allows frequent listening, tuning and adjustment. There is no value in letting a team make catastrophic mistakes before realizing that change is needed. As coaches, facilitators, educators, we can guide teams to early recognition of warning signs. We can, and we do. That is why people engage us in this work.

My thoughts on personal change have less clarity. Having been through my own catastrophic personal changes, I know it is not to be desired. I also know that sometimes that's just the way it is, and coming through the other side of that change can be a profound and awakening experience. Most of us don't have personal coaches to guide our thinking and behaviors in the way we can guide teams—and would we listen, even if we did? Most of us do not make visible what is going on internally. We perceive that as weakness. We mask, we bluff, we talk the talk. We build facades and we find ways to hide our vulnerability and our mistakes, and we even cover for others, to avoid conflict. We like things to be nice. And therein lie the ingredients for a catastrophe. The majority of us will not see a psychotherapist, a spiritual guide, a marriage guidance counselor, or even a doctor until we reach crisis point—often crisis-bordering-on-catastrophe. Admitting defeat is too devastating a proposition.

I think it is human nature to deny problems. We are a hopeful species. Look at Hurricane Katrina. It was known that Lake Pontchartrain's levees were weak; it was known they might collapse… but drawing analogies with natural disasters is not always helpful. The point is, with good guidance and early intervention catastrophe can be avoided. In our personal lives, to some extent, and with teams, to a greater extent, we have the ability to intercept. What about at the organizational level? That's tougher.

At the team and individual level, we are dealing with people—people we can meet, talk to, get to know. At the organizational level we cease dealing with people. Organizations are amorphous blobs, sometimes huge ones. They resemble those strange sea creatures you see in Jacques Cousteau documentaries, where you can't distinguish the face from the anus. Many such creatures may not even have a central nervous system. There may be a person in charge of the blob, but so often that is in name only, and usually that person is answerable to a board of directors, and then to shareholders, who are all so far removed from the day-to-day process, from the passion, as to be unreachable. Which orifice of the blob do we address ourselves to? Who, or what, makes the change decisions?

Catastrophic organizational change doesn't come about because we choose it; it comes about because the knowledge of how to introduce sustainable change into a large organization is not yet well known. That's how it is. We are on a voyage of discovery.

Organizational change is a very, very different animal to team change and personal change. Each type of change needs to be considered in its own context. We do each one a disservice by grouping it with the others, and assuming the issues can be addressed with a single strategy.

Personal change often needs a very individual awakening to occur, and that will be different for each person. As facilitators we can provide creative space to inform and guide that process, but we cannot make it happen.

From a team perspective, I believe the short-span inspect/adapt model of "crisis and victory" is the correct way to proceed as we introduce agile thinking and behaviors into big organizations, but I don't think we should fool ourselves into thinking that the success we see at the team level will ripple up through the organization in a similar, healthy way. I predict it will not.

December 15, 2005

In a Roundabout Sort of Way

I recently moved to a new apartment, and almost every day I am obliged to drive to and from my home via an incomprehensible junction. I quickly grew exasperated enough to tweet out loud: "The city of Palo Alto misses the point. A roundabout with stop signs is like a self-organizing team with a manager." Figuring I wasn't the first person to find this arrangement ridiculous, I decided to read a little more about roundabouts, so common in Europe, so sparse in the USA (and so sadly misunderstood in Palo Alto).

I found a wonderfully informative resource, published by the Insurance Institute for Highway Safety (IIHS),[1] which describes the benefits (and the few limitations) of roundabouts. Road planning is an intriguing metaphor for organizational culture.

Stop signs represent a controlling, and mistrustful system. In Palo Alto, there are stop signs on almost every junction... but not every junction. This simply causes confusion to all but long-term residents, and makes the potential for accidents high. It's as if we are forever being told what to do, and then all of a sudden someone says, "Oh, just do what you like." Eek! Every time I cross one of those rare intersections I am afraid that the person coming at right angles to me isn't aware that I have the right of way. Tiny lettering on an otherwise identical sign tells him "two way stop." Will he read it? I have no idea; I'll assume not.

[1] The Insurance Institute for Highway Safety, iihs.org

People cannot be trusted in an environment where mistrust is cultivated.

Wouldn't it be interesting if there were no stop signs at all? I'd like to see a city which simply trusts that people will drive responsibly, and provides some guides to assist in that process (roundabouts, road bumps, etc.). After all, most people would like to not die in a road accident. Before you cry "No, no! That could never work!" take a look at the statistics. We already know that the introduction of roundabouts seriously reduces intersection collisions, for example:

> *Studies of intersections in Europe and Australia that were converted to roundabouts have reported...45-75 percent reductions in severe injury crashes.*[2]

Interesting. It seems that trusting drivers to be responsible, rather than keeping them under strict control, actually saves lives. I wonder what the "crash-rate" statistics of command-and-control companies look like. Will agile be the roundabout of the corporate world?

Roundabouts are common throughout Europe, with 30,000 roundabouts in France alone by 2010, and many more outside Europe in countries such as Australia, New Zealand, United Arab Emirates, Qatar, Malaysia and Costa Rica. What happened in the USA to leave them so far behind the rest of the world in terms of the way they manage their traffic flow? In part, the problem lies with a deep cultural resistance to change. The *New York Times* called roundabouts "the bane of many drivers' existence" in 2007.[3]

The *New York Times* later furnished some actual figures: "All told, there are about 2,000 roundabouts in [the USA], most built in the last decade", and went on to quote Eugene R. Russell Sr., a

[2] Q & A Roundabouts, IIHS (iihs.org/research/qanda/roundabouts.aspx)
[3] Jill P. Capuzzo, "A Shift, but for Some Drivers, a Vicious Circle," *New York Times*, November 25, 2007

civil engineering professor at Kansas State University and chairman of a national task force on roundabouts as saying, "There's a lot of what I call irrational opposition...People don't understand. They just don't understand roundabouts." [4]

I started wondering what this resistance was about. Why do US city planners resist, while those in other countries so readily embrace this concept. Is it resistance to outside ideas, the inability to make quick decisions, or is it a reluctance to release power? And then I read the IIHS's take on the impediments to building roundabouts:

> *Despite the safety and other benefits of roundabouts, as well as the high levels of public acceptance once they are built, some states and cities have been slow to build roundabouts, and some are even opposed to building them. The principal impediment is the negative perception held by some drivers and elected officials. Transportation agencies also have long been accustomed to installing traffic signals, and it can take time for deeply rooted design practices to change.*[5]

How apt. This can minimally be rephrased for our context: Despite the improved productivity and other benefits of agile, as well as the higher levels of customer satisfaction once products are built, some organizations have been slow to embrace agile, and some are even opposed to adopting the ideas. The principle impediment is the negative perception held by some developers and managers. Traditional businesses also have long been accustomed to installing controlling processes, and it can take time for deeply rooted management practices to change.

August 18th, 2009

[4] Andrew Keh, "European Import Has Cars Spinning. Heads, Too," *New York Times*, November 18, 2010

[5] Q & A Roundabouts, IIHS (iihs.org/research/qanda/roundabouts.aspx)

The Change Agent's Blade is Thin and Keen

Cutting Up an Ox

By Chuang Tzu

Prince Wen Hui's cook
Was cutting up an ox.
Out went a hand,
Down went a shoulder,
He planted a foot,
He pressed with a knee
The ox fell apart
With a whisper,
The bright cleaver murmured
Like a gentle wind.
Rhythm! Timing!
Like a sacred dance,
Like "The Mulberry Grove"
Like ancient harmonies!

"Good work!" the Prince exclaimed,
"Your method is faultless!"
"Method?" said the cook
Laying aside his cleaver,
"What I follow is Tao
Beyond all methods!

"When I first began
To cut up oxen
I would see before me
The whole ox
All in one mass.

"After three years
I no longer saw this mass.
I saw the distinctions.

"But now, I see nothing
With the eye. My whole being
Apprehends.
My senses are idle. The spirit
Free to work without plan
Follows its own instinct
Guided by natural line,
By the secret opening,
The hidden space,
My cleaver finds its own way.
I cut through no joint, chop no bone.

"A great cook needs a new chopper
Once a year - he cuts.
A poor cook needs a new one
Every month - he hacks!

"I have used this same cleaver
Nineteen years.
It has cut up
A thousand oxen.
Its edge is as keen
As if newly sharpened.

"There are spaces in the joints;
The blade is thin and keen:

When this thinness
Finds that space
There is all the room you need!
It goes like a breeze!
Hence I have this cleaver
Nineteen years
As if newly sharpened!

"True, there are sometimes
Tough joints. I feel them coming,
I slow down, I watch closely,
Hold back, barely move the blade,
And whump! the part falls away
Landing like a clod of earth.

"Then I withdraw the blade,
I stand still
And let the joy of the work
Sink in.
I clean the blade
And put it away."

Prince Wen Hui said,
"This is it! My cook has shown me
How I ought to live
My own life!"

I have long admired the above Taoist poem, *Cutting Up an Ox* [1] by Chuang Tzu and recently recognized in it a pattern for how I'd like to introduce agility into an organization. The poem really speaks for itself in explaining this, but I'll add a few words of commentary to put it into context.

An organization, on first encounter, appears as one mass—or blob, as described in a previous chapter. Through working with the individuals—especially, but certainly not exclusively, with

[1] The version of the poem reproduced here is from The Way of Chuang Tzu, pp 45-48, by Thomas Merton (New York: New Directions, 1969)

those at a grassroots level—the distinctions become apparent. Lines, channels of communication, begin to emerge and communication blocks are unearthed. The organizational flow (or lack thereof) becomes apparent.

At this stage it is tempting to believe that the solutions are obvious, and there is a strong desire to go in with advice and start to change things. This is perhaps too soon. Like the cook in the poem, we need to wait until we "see nothing," but begin to apprehend in a new way altogether. Then perhaps the solutions will find themselves. Life flows.

Given the space, given trust, people will inevitably behave in the right way; it is in our natures to seek harmony. When the knife blade is "'thin and keen," it almost doesn't hurt at all: it is invisible. As coaches, perhaps all we need to do is pause, barely move the blade, and simply watch the barriers fall away. That place of readiness will not be reached without time and trust, and there is much groundwork to be done to prepare the path.

The process begins with quiet listening; it does not begin with loud instruction.

December 23, 2005

Scrum Adoption: The Awakening

What does it take for an organization to fundamentally change the way it works and embrace a new way of being, in particular a pathway as radically different as scrum? I believe it requires an awakening, which manifests itself in three ways, interwoven and complimentary: Honesty, open-mindedness and willingness. Those familiar with the treatment of addiction will recognize these qualities as being the necessary requirements for an addict to seek recovery.[1] Drug addicts, dysfunctional software organizations... not as different as one might think.

The first requirement: Honesty

A broken organization, one that is suffering from the overhead and dehumanization of a command-and-control culture—embarked upon, no doubt, for the best of reasons and a belief that such an approach would yield the best results—needs first to admit complete defeat. This takes a profound level of honesty that few possess. Of course, what it means for "an organization" to admit defeat is really for those in charge to do so. But the leadership is not solely to be blamed, perhaps every member of the organization, every employee needs to take responsibility. There needs to be an overall sense of "we're done with this." Without such an admission of defeat, few organizations will honestly seek a new way of working, and will instead look for quick fixes to their existing processes, believing that if only

[1] Narcotics Anonymous, World Service Office, 1984

people would work harder, do as they are told, if managers were stricter, more in control, then everything would work according to plan.

Don't get me wrong. I don't mean that every organization must be on the point of going broke and closing down in order to adopt scrum. An addict doesn't have to be on death's door to begin the process of recovery. Hitting bottom is a personal thing. I once knew a recovering addict who when asked how he knew he had hit bottom, replied "I stopped digging." When we stop digging we can focus on what is beyond the hole. We get to look at the stars.

The second requirement: Open-mindedness

Once an organization honestly admits the path it is on is the wrong one, it immediately opens its collective mind to the possibility of something different. This is a leap of faith, especially when that 'something different' is as yet unknown. Being open-minded to a new direction that we can only as yet identify as "not this thing" is a scary proposition. Many organizations have heard of scrum and other agile frameworks, but often the reports are riddled with inaccuracies. They are likely to be a cocktail of myth, fact, horror stories of anarchy and developer rebellion, mocking tales of new age hippies making everyone hold hands and share their feelings, exaggerated claims of 10x productivity and unlikely promises of "faster, better, cheaper." It takes a lot of courage, or a state of despair, to stay open-minded in the face of the unknown.

The third requirement: Willingness

An organization that has admitted failure, and whose only shot at redemption is something as radical and misunderstood as scrum, faces a real dilemma—can't go back, dare not go forward. Without a willingness to attempt something different, the only place to go is nowhere. The organization can trudge on in the same old way, slowly sinking as more lightweight competitors rise up and capture the market, or they can change. We are not necessarily willing by choice, but sometimes through lack of any better alternative. Sometimes the adoption of scrum will come not from "Hey that sounds great!" but rather "What the heck." Either way, the willingness to at least explore this new paradigm gives hope where before there was only frustration and despair.

These three qualities alone are not sufficient, but I believe they are necessary for an organization to reach a state of awareness, to be able to explore scrum in a holistic way. Again, total failure isn't a requirement, just the desire to stop digging, to stop acting in the same old ways expecting different results. Those who have no desire to change, who want to use scrum as a quick fix, a patch to their existing processes while remaining locked in old thinking and arrogance will get exactly what they seek: a duct tape solution, temporary and non-sustainable. Those who start their journey with an honest admission of defeat, an openness to new ideas, and a willingness to embrace a new paradigm will stand a better chance of long-term success. In some coaching circles this is known as a breakdown. But the sense of powerlessness and impotence we face in this breakdown is temporary. The world of knowledge work is changing; those willing to let go of old ideas and embrace this change will quickly discover a new power—a very different kind of power rooted in respect, trust, and a passion for creation.

Once an organization is willing to embrace what scrum has to offer its people will need to spring into action to start building their scrum organization.[2] They will need help. This help is available from consultants, of course, but more importantly it is available in the wider agile community.

[2] I'd like to make it clear that I am using scrum as an example of a radically different approach to work. More broadly, it is the concept of an empirical, self-organized, collaborative approach with flattened hierarchies and worker autonomy that is so daunting to many traditional thinkers.

Seek out a local agile group, or join an online agile forum. Meet fellow travelers in different stages of organizational recovery and find out what they did to overcome their impediments. Tapping into the collective agile conscience will help you. Be prepared to begin by embracing not only the scrum framework, but its underlying values and principles too—a key one being the building of a trusting, self-organized community within your organization. The scrum framework/process alone will only serve as a band-aid solution. A true transformation will need a deep wound cleansing, and quite possibly a spiritual awakening. No one is saying this is easy.

July 3rd, 2010

Team Culture, Project Culture

I've heard a lot over the years about how scrum is inadequate for managing large projects—some would say managing projects at all—and much has been written about the need for agile project management, or the implementation of a lean or kanban approach to mitigate this apparent inadequacy. Broken scrum implementations are (we hear) fixed by the addition of one or more of these approaches, or even by combining scrum with a defined (e.g. waterfall) approach. I don't doubt the case studies. In fact, I agree that scrum is a half-baked way to manage projects.

But what's interesting here is that we stay stuck in the idea that projects must be managed—or even that there need be projects at all. While we hold on to our project-centric mindset scrum will never be an appropriate solution—and I'd argue that none of the other suggested alternatives or enhancements will be much better. As long as we try to add layers of agility onto what is essentially an incompatible foundation, we will only ever see limited success—and quick reversion back to status quo at the slightest panic. For any truly agile effort to work, we need a complete paradigm shift in how we approach business.

Back in the 1970s, or perhaps earlier, the software world adopted what we might call a "project culture." This means that the project is king, and the people are there to serve the project. Projects have managers, and if we add more managers we can add more projects, and get more things done at once. So goes the thinking. And what follows is that people become "resources" to the projects. It is the individual contributor who is sought after by the competing project managers, whose attention is frequently tugged in multiple directions, and teams—such as they are in a project culture—are weak entities, frequently broken apart as priorities change and skill-sets are needed elsewhere.

The project culture undermines a key principle of effective workmanship: that of focus. When individuals are pushed from project to project a massive overhead of context switching and thus loss of productivity is incurred. In simple context-switching experiments I've run with small groups this cost runs around 30-50%. I'm sure it is much higher in complex environments. Because of this mess we have to hire more managers to better "level the resources." Moving people around, assigning work, tracking that work, all this needs careful and detailed management, and good project managers are not cheap. The project culture creates problems that we seek to solve by enforcing the project culture. Reminds me of noted "software psychologist" Gerald Weinberg's first rule of bad management: If something isn't working, do more of it.[1]

An alternative to project culture is team culture. In a team culture, the teams are multi-skilled and stable, and this stability leads to enhanced focus and high performance.[2] In a team culture, individuals are not assigned to projects—and more interestingly, neither are teams. There is no assignment. Teams take the lead here—they pull work in, as appropriate to their skill set and areas of interest. You can picture a company's projects (or products, sub-products, features) displayed visually in rough order of priority, for all the teams to see. When a team completes a project, it selects another one—one appropriate to the skills and interests of the team's members.

[1] Gerald M. Weinberg, *Quality Software Management: Vol. 1 Systems Thinking* (New York: Dorset House Publishing, 1992)
[2] Bruce Wayne Tuckman, "Developmental Sequence in Small Groups," *Psychology Bulletin*, June 1965

Ideally, projects (like stories) will be made as small as possible; the term minimal marketable feature (MMF) is often used for these small chunks of functionality. One team may take on many MMF's towards a greater product goal, or multiple teams may work on the same product, pulling in the MMFs that are appropriate to their skills. It doesn't matter how this is done, provided we work in a reflective way, aligning frequently with customers and users. If the teams take the lead, the job will get done well. The principle of self-organization says that the people doing the work are the best people to decide how to do the work. And that includes knowing which work they should be doing in the first place.

Team culture offers a simple approach to solving complex problems. It cuts down on unnecessary people-management overhead and fosters a more focused approach to work. Confronting the context switching madness in this way has a two-fold reward: i) it eliminates busy work—which is waste, thus leading to more products being completed in less time, and ii) workers are engaged in a healthy, inspiring way. The elimination of busy work also opens up the opportunity for slack time,[3] where developers can sharpen their tools, research, invent, and play. Companies that allow such freedoms tend to do better than those that keep their workers' noses to the grindstone. Google, with their famous policy of giving engineers 20% of their time to "work on something...that interests them personally," is an example of a company that created phenomenal success through the practice of release and trust.[4]

I believe scrum fosters team culture—at least it is a good starting point. Scrum begins with cross-functional teams accepting work of a transactional nature and seeking completion before

[3] Tom DeMarco, *Slack: Getting Past Burnout, Busywork, and the Myth of Total Efficiency* (New York: Crown Business, 2002)
[4] Bharat Mediratta, "The Google Way: Give Engineers Room," *New York Times*, October 21, 2007.

moving on to the next thing. The timebox limits the amount of work a team can take on. Effective teams generally use the kanban principle of limited work in progress (WIP),[5] working on only a very few transactional stories at one time. Some teams choose not to commit at all, but simply pull in stories according to their WIP limit, being careful not to start something that cannot be finished in a sprint. The important thing here is not whether teams make commitments, or how they make them, but that these are cross-functional teams that collaborate with requesters, manage their own time and process, and focus on the completion of work.

If organizations wanting to adopt scrum would be willing to shift from a project culture to a team culture, they'd find that many of the problems associated with project management would disappear. They would reduce (project) management overhead costs, stop calling in consultants to fix whatever the previous consultants screwed up, and see a stream-lined, effective organization emerging right before their eyes. Trust the teams. It's as simple—and terrifying—as that.

April 17th, 2012

[5] Limited WIP is based on the lean principle of one-piece flow, and adapted from a manufacturing paradigm to a software one. It is essentially a watered-down version of one-piece flow (it can be thought of as some-pieces flow) as most software companies have traditionally encouraged narrow skill sets, making true one-piece flow difficult, and often economically unviable. Limiting work in progress encourages team members to expand their skill set and collaborate with one another on fewer work items at a time, perhaps eventually getting to true one-piece flow.

Don’t Build Teams

In their spiritual classic, *Compassion, A Reflection on the Christian Life,*[1] authors Nouwen, McNeill, and Morrison write:

> *...the question arises, “How can we build community? What do we have to do to make community happen?” But perhaps such questions come from an anxious heart and are less practical and helpful than they appear to be. It seems better to raise the more contemplative question, “Where do we see community occurring?”*

This insightful question brings to mind a parallel in organizations looking to take on scrum as a way to mend, or to improve. The question arises among executives and managers, “How do we build a team? How do we know who to put on which team?” Perhaps what they are really asking is, “How can we guarantee success?”

My usual answer is, don’t build teams, let teams emerge. Nouwen et al.’s wording for this is much more powerful, and focused. They advise that we simply observe what is. We can contextualize the question for corporate managers by recasting it as, “Where do we see team occurring?” This question could be very revealing, for if we don’t see team occurring in our organization it suggests we have deeper problems of engagement, autonomy, collaboration and trust. When these values are missing, tacking on something we think will “improve our process” has little meaning, and will undoubtedly—and expensively—fail.

[1] Henri Nouwen, Donald P. McNeill, and Douglas A. Morrison, *Compassion, a Reflection on the Christian Life* (New York: Doubleday, 1982)

Is team occurring in your organization? Here are a few things to look out for: people leaving their cubicles for long periods of time to work side-by-side with others; heated dialog relating to a product or method of implementation; cross-functional conversations—developers spending time with testers, and vice versa; spontaneous public acknowledgement of another's work or ideas; laughter; argument; dissent; awkward questions; group lunches; respectful listening; appreciation; direct confrontation (rather than indirect complaining); hurt; anger; frustration. While not all these traits are seen as positive, it is very likely they all indicate some level of engagement—of caring about the work and caring about others. Look to what can be embraced and nurtured.

If your organization consists of quiet, obedient, perhaps even efficient workers, waiting for their next assignment and handing off work to others, compliant people, doing what is asked of them without question, people keeping their heads down, staying silent for fear of reprisal, then you will probably not see team occurring. The question then becomes, "How do we release people?"—a question that needs to come a few eons before the "How do we create team?" question.

February 26th, 2012

Scaling Scrum: The Alcoholic Perspective

Scaling agile is the last thing you want to do.

—*Martin Fowler*[1]

Everybody wants to scale scrum. It seems like one of the first questions asked in many scrum introductory courses. Day one, 11am: "Yes, but how can I make this work with 5,000 people across 27 world-wide locations?" This is understandable. There is a desire, especially among software professionals—to seek quick solutions to hugely complex problems, but if we do that before understanding the basics we are unlikely to make good decisions.

Learn about scrum, I mean really learn, before jumping to impossible scenarios and expecting scrum to have pat answers. Software engineers are bright people, sometimes too bright. We praise those who can leap ahead with their thinking, who skip steps; we look to them as the smartest of us all. But scrum does not benefit from step-skipping, it benefits more from a one-foot-in-front-of the-other approach, the learning occurring along the way.

I believe scrum to be self-scaling. By that, I mean that scrum contains all the elements required for handling complexity: self-organization, empiricism, prioritization and timeboxing. Scaling

[1] Martin Fowler, "Why Scaling Agile Is the Last Thing You Want to Do", keynote speech at the 1st Canadian Agile Network Workshop, Banff, Alberta, Canada, February 2003

scrum does not benefit from interference, but rather from support and understanding. Develop a deep and thorough appreciation of the scrum principles and practices. This will allow you (as manager, director, scrum master) to step back and allow scaling to happen according to scrum principles, rather than to fit your own perceived patterns of what is right. Don't attempt to influence the change, but gently guide it to meet specific organizational and team needs. In other words: Get out of the way.

One interesting parallel for self-organized scaling comes from the world of self-help groups: In 1935 Bill Wilson and Dr. Bob Smith formed a group in Akron, Ohio to help alcoholics like themselves recover from the obsession, or disease of alcoholism. From this small, self-organized group (there were no therapists, counselors or leaders) grew an entire, world-wide movement now known as Alcoholics Anonymous. How did this happen? How were a bunch of ex-drunks able to apply the principles of self-organized scaling to their movement without someone being in charge? The answer is that the solution emerged slowly, and according to need.

Bill Wilson eventually moved back to New York, and being unable to attend meetings of his newly formed Akron group he began a second, local group. This group grew too, and a similar thing happened. Groups formed from a common beginning, according to the needs (usually geographical) of the members. Groups dissolved too, when the need was no longer there. Eventually a few people had the idea that a set of guiding principles would be useful to give an overall sense of cohesion to the disparate groups and thus a set of "traditions" was established by a loose collective of people from many different groups.[2] Among the guiding principles in these traditions are the following:

Our leaders are but trusted servants; they do not govern.

[2] The 12 Traditions of Alcoholics Anonymous, © 1946, AA World Services, NYC.

> *Each group should be autonomous except in matters affecting other groups or AA as a whole.*
>
> *Each group has but one primary purpose—to carry its message to the alcoholic who still suffers.*

It will easily be seen how such principles can apply to the scaling of scrum:

> *Our leaders are but trusted servants; they do not govern.* [No change there.]
>
> *Each team should be autonomous except in matters affecting other teams or the organization as a whole.*
>
> *Each team has but one primary purpose—to build an increment of product in every iteration and deliver it to the customer (who is possibly suffering!).*
>
> It may be argued that this example is too far removed from the world of software to be useful. Perhaps you are thinking that recovering alcoholics are not responsible for deadlines and deliveries. But think again. Without AA many of those alcoholics would be dead. Avoiding death is probably the best deadline of all! There is certainly a sense of urgency that permeates AA meetings. It is a last refuge for many: We recover together or we die alone. Don't be too quick to dismiss the parallel here on the argument of non-relevance. It is the scaling of an idea in an emergent, self-organized way that is of interest. Seek out the similarities in this model, rather than focusing on the differences.

April 9th, 2008

Seeking Consent

...consensus is good, decisions are better. Hear from every voice, but don't be held hostage by consensus

— *Michael Spayd (@mspayd)*

Most people just suck at getting consensus. Maybe we should improve that skill instead of promoting exclusion

— *Derek Neighbors (@dneighbors)*

This short dialog on Twitter caught my attention. Consensus has long been a topic of discussion in the agile community, and these statements seem to capture the two dominant trains of thought: Those who believe that consensus is the most effective way to avoid conflict and disagreement, to ensure all are "on board" with the decisions reached; and those who believe consensus holds back decision-making, who advocate for strong leaders stepping in when people are unable to agree. Neither idea appeals to me.

Rarely do large groups of people all agree on even something as low-risk as where to have lunch, so finding agreement on product goals or development strategy is thus highly unlikely. I understand Spayd's argument, which says, "Let's have a leader who will ultimately make the call." The problem with that approach is that over time, the minority voice will become silenced, and the minority speakers disillusioned and disempowered. Is there another way forward?

I am reminded of the concept of consent, as described by the

19th Century French philosopher Auguste Comte, one of the founding thinkers of sociocracy,[1] a radical theory of governance still popular with eco-villages, co-housing projects and forward-thinking companies around the world. While consensus is usually understood as "everyone is in agreement," consent is more like, "no one is opposed"—or in sociocratic terms, "there are no paramount objections." This is an important distinction. Consent isn't agreement, and it isn't approval. When a father gives his consent for his daughter to marry, he doesn't necessarily agree with or approve of her choice, but his consent concedes that he is willing to trust her, and thus offers release. Excuse the archaic analogy; it helps illustrate the principle. Consent is about letting go of self and trusting others. It can only be done if the trust has previously been established; if not it can take some time to get there.

In the western world we hold up democracy as the utmost exemplar of a fair system. Everyone has a voice, and the majority (the loudest voice) wins. But where there are winners, there are losers, and where there are losers there is disgruntlement. The following passage from Barbara Kingsolver's marvelous novel, *The Poisonwood Bible*,[2] set during the formation of the Democratic Republic of the Congo in 1960, explains the downside of democracy while neatly, albeit accidentally, outlining the sociocratic model of circular organizing. The narrator speaks of Tata Ngu, the tribal leader of the village of Kilanga:

> *Whatever we might think of this imposing man in his pointed hat, he is a figurehead who represents the will of Kilanga. I believe that is why Brother Fowles said we should respect him, or at least pay attention, no matter how out-of-whack the chief might seem. He's not just speaking for himself. Every few weeks Tata Ndu has meetings with his sous-chiefs, who have their own*

[1] Gerard Endenbu, *Sociocracy: The organization of decision-making* (Delft: Eburon, 1998)
[2] Barbara Kingsolver, The Poisonwood Bible (New York: HarperCollins 1998)

meetings with all the families. So by the time Tata Ndu gets around to saying something, you can be pretty sure the whole village is talking to you.

Anatole has been explaining to me the native system of government. He says the whole business of throwing pebbles into bowls with the most pebbles winning an election—that was Belgium's idea of fair play, to the people here it is peculiar. To the Congolese (including Anatole himself, he confessed) it seems odd that if one man gets fifty votes and the other gets forty-nine, the first one wins altogether and the second one plumb loses. That means almost half the people will be unhappy, and according to Anatole, in a village that's left halfway unhappy you haven't heard the end of it. There is sure to be trouble somewhere down the line.

Are decisions really better when many are left unhappy? I don't think so. In our rush to do things, to see results, we leave a trail of unhappiness. As Neighbors pointed out, most of us are not good at reaching consensus, but that shouldn't be an excuse to practice exclusion. Exclusion hurts. We should seek to get better at hearing the common voice rather than silencing those who object.

I can hear the opposition to this: "But we'll never get anything done!" I don't buy it. I have witnessed the sociocratic consent process in action, and it is actually beautiful—deeply frustrating sometimes, but beautiful because it creates community instead of division, and when things get done they are done with care and respect for the whole community, not through the oppression of the minority.

At times we may actually be better off doing nothing, but simply being—i.e. taking time to explore who we are and what we care about, to understand our true desires and those of our fellows, and to listen to where the pain lies, where anger may be festering. If we embrace the dissonance of the group and seek understanding, seek to listen rather than persuade, then perhaps the decisions we ultimately make will come from a place of peace, and thus be in the best interest of the entire community.

Consent requires trust; trust is achieved through understanding; understanding emerges from listening; and listening requires silence. If you want your voice to be truly heard, stop talking.

August 18th, 2012

The Spirit of Change

Many of my engagements as an agile consultant begin with a request from an executive or management team to "improve development." The focus of these organizations is essentially: "Fix my people." But the people don't need fixing; they are usually highly skilled, intelligent individuals caught up in a crappy system. It isn't people we need to fix; it is systems.

Now, I've known this for a while, but one particular engagement brought it home to me in a way I was no longer willing to ignore. I found myself in an organization rich with bright, passionate people blossoming with great ideas and desperate for the freedom to be the greatest they could be, but thoroughly beaten down by an executive team caught up in 1980s style management, characterized by blustering, threatening, underhanded behavior. No trust existed in either direction, people were being laid off without warning, and others departed in despair. All this I was expected to fix with a two-day scrum training and a couple of weeks of consulting.

As a consultant there are times when my integrity is seriously challenged. This was one of those times. It took all of two days to accurately assess the situation, and yet I chose to stay the full two weeks, despite the knowledge that I could change very little, if anything, about the way this organization operated. My excuses ranged from the very cynical, "I'm here now, I may as well get paid for it," to the more humane, "Maybe I can help the individuals recognize a better way of working and find their way out of this place."

At the end of the short engagement I was asked to come back

again at a later date. This sounded hopeful, but not if it was to help perpetuate the myth that the problem lay in the people. It was very apparent the problem lay in the system—or perhaps more accurately, that it lay in the people who created and perpetuated the system, i.e. the executives—the ones who wouldn't give me half an hour of their time in the whole two weeks I was there to talk about their part in the dysfunction. If I was to come back I had to insist on some real change measures to address the systemic issues. My proposal included training and coaching with executives, coaching with sales and product teams, dialogs with HR to confront the hiring and rewards policies, and very little about fixing developers and making them do scrum. I was not invited back.

It was around this time I made the decision to quit consulting, and to seek a more permanent role inside an organization where, perhaps over years, I could influence some real change at a deep, systemic level. I was never going to be able to do that as a hired gun.

To be fair to the company I mention here, they are not alone. Far from it. They are merely one instance of a massive lie that is perpetuated in business: more control equals better profits. This astounding myth plays out over and over again, even sadly, in new startups. Decades of research into what motivates people is simply ignored, perhaps so those in charge can feel important in their positional power, to the extent they can muster an illusion of control.

W. Edwards Deming observed over forty years ago that in any work environment the system itself is 85% of the problem, the people a mere 15%.[1] And yet we continue to ignore this observation, putting all our focus on measuring, rewarding, punishing, and monitoring the people. How misguided. Companies everywhere, but perhaps in the knowledge industry even more so, are

[1] This proportion varies from 80/20 to 95/5 depending on which source is referenced. The point doesn't change: the problems of an organization lie overwhelmingly in the system.

made up of good people. Good in all respects of the word: skilled at their jobs, kind-hearted, fair-minded; they want success for themselves, their teams and their organizations as a whole. And yet there is much pain and frustration in the workplace. The systems we work in are broken; they are remnants of a time past—heavy, outmoded, and ignorant of human psychology. Even knowing this, we stand in silent witness while senior management in these organizations (good people themselves, also lost in the system) continue to seek to fix the people; they use reward and punishment strategies deeply embedded in the culture to attempt to motivate demotivated individuals; they bring in consultants (like me) to offer band-aid solutions like agile and its flavors of the moment: scrum and kanban. But it's not band-aids we need, it is major surgery, or perhaps psychotherapy.

A colleague and fellow consultant, Bob Marshall, has coined the term organizational therapy to describe his own work: "Organizational therapy offers a non-directive approach to addressing some of the dysfunctions present in any organization. It allows the organization to grow in self-awareness and capability by seeing itself more clearly, and then finding its own solutions to some of its more pressing issues." [2]

I see his point. The work we need to do is about getting to the root of the problem, uncovering the uncomfortable, facing demons, each of us owning our own part in this dysfunction we call business. At one time the agile movement looked like a way out of this mess, but for all its fanfares, conferences, tools, promotions, corporate blustering, and even its uppercase "A", agile as a movement has proven itself incapable of such profound alteration. It's time to cast aside this facade of change and own up to failure.

Agility is a vague, abstract idea, made concrete through its implementations—essentially extreme programming, scrum, and

[2] Bob Marshall, *Think Different* (flowchainsensei.wordpress.com)

kanban. There is much good in each of these implementation frameworks—a creative edginess that begins to challenge old thinking—but inevitably the corporatization of agile has slowly chipped away at this edge, rounding it nicely to fit to the existing status quo. Worse, many so-called agilists embrace this as "a good thing," exalting in the burgeoning mainstream acceptance of agile. As a community we are so caught up in promoting our ideas, preaching at conferences, writing books, making money, that we have lost sight—if we ever had it in the first place—of what really matters.

This is what matters to me: engagement, love, passion, excitement, release, freedom, personal responsibility, courage, inquisitiveness, laughter, life—spirit! No framework or process will give us spirit, no clever tool that drags and drops virtual sticky notes, no buzz words, and certainly no hard-sell consulting company making promises of change while complying with the existing cultural dysfunction and raking in the monetary rewards. Spirit comes from within, and it is actualized through service to something bigger than ourselves. Until we start seeking such actualization, each one of us, we will be bound by blind procedure, vacuous promise and despair.

I'm done with uppercase Agile, and its associated sales pitches and empty promises. Instead I'll embrace true agility—elegant, curious, and lighthearted. I'm done with directives and defined outcomes. Instead I'll be more willing to say, "I have no idea—let's explore." I'm done with compliance to harsh, angry hierarchies, to the worship of false idols. Instead I want to approach my work with an open heart, a beginner's mind and an anarchist's soul. The wisdom to embrace change and the capacity for true human engagement resides in each of us individually, as well as in our collective consciousness. My job—if I have one at all—is only to open the cage doors, sever the ties that bind us to a dead culture, and clear the space. If chaos ensues, that's all to the good. As self-organizing systems, each team, group or enterprise will converge on a way of working, a way of being, that best suits its needs. Trust in the inherent goodness of ourselves and our colleagues, and a heartfelt desire to make the world a better place, for this is all we need to begin. The rest will emerge.

October 1st, 2012

Afterword

By Lyssa Adkins

As you may have experienced for yourself as you read this book, one of Tobias Mayer's signature moves is to pick up a stone and throw it through our glass house, smashing our old paradigms and causing us, after some pain and turmoil, to say, "OK, my comfortable way doesn't work anymore. Now what?"

There was a time, a few years ago, when I was frequently teaching the Certified ScrumMaster class and the inevitable question would arise every class, "Can you do scrum with geographically distributed teams? You know, the ones where our testers are a half-day ahead of us?" I would start the conversation by putting up a long quote from one of Tobias' essays that begins, "Distributed teams are not teams..." You probably read it in this book, on page 34. As the students read, I watched a sense of futility seep into the expressions on their faces. I felt despair creep into the room. Their glass houses had been shattered.

Perhaps surprisingly, I never once had anyone argue with Tobias' words, because they so cuttingly gave voice to the human experience of trying to work inside a system that doesn't support our best work. Then, instead of giving the students a pep talk or trying to reassure them, I worked with the futility and the despair. I helped them pick up their shards of glass and answer the question, "Now what?" This led to a rich dialog about how scrum can help an organization overcome decisions that once seemed smart but now block our best efforts—how scrum can help an organization be great. This painful yet honest conversation would not have happened if we started off by "being nice" and talking about how to twist scrum to accommodate the way things currently are.

This is just one example of how Tobias' writings have influenced me and the thousands of people I have worked with. His work is more than skin deep. It cuts right to the core.

That's probably why I have heard people call Tobias a maverick, a firebrand and an anarchist—as well as a few other unsavory things better left unsaid. You may have had some of those reactions yourself. Think about it: What is it about this man—who is, after all, writing about nothing more controversial than business—that provokes this kind of passion in people (and maybe in you)? Surely, it's several attributes, but perhaps the forcefulness of his ideas is the key one. He pulls no punches which makes it hard for us readers to stay neutral. He evokes strong reactions that push us off the fence one way or the other, whether or not we like it, and whether or not we feel ready for it.

Most of the essays in this book began as blog posts, and the back-and-forth discourse that they originally agitated among those of us who read and regularly commented on them created a deeper understanding of what's happening beneath agile. Ultimately, these battles lit the way for many of us to answer our own "Now what?"

I am excited to see these groundbreaking essays all in one place, and in such a beautifully-crafted vessel as *The People's Scrum*. Readers of his blog will benefit from having them pulled together into one well-organized thought form, and those who are encountering him for the first time will have their appetites whetted for more. It's a good thing, too, because Tobias does not stop. Once these ideas are metabolized, he has even more in store for us.

This book neatly sets the stage for his latest work on business craftsmanship, where Tobias elevates the discussion even further and takes us into innovative social and emotional right-brain landscapes that give meaning to our next-generation organizations and networks. I agree with Tobias that scrum is participating in an evolution toward models taken from nature, and away from the machine model errantly stamped all over our current business world. We are just beginning to see it, gleaming in the distance. Tobias reveals it and helps us see it in his business craftsmanship writings. In this way he is not a mere paradigm breaker, but a paradigm builder, giving us access to the new ways of working just now emerging. And although he's building rather than smashing this time around, I'm pretty sure he'll still find ways to shock us (for our own good).

Appendix I: Scrum

A Simple Framework for Solving Complex Problems

Scrum as a concept is almost impossibly simple—too simple it seems—for the often brilliant and always complex people expected to embrace it. Scrum frequently gets over-complicated by zealous process-engineers and those raised in the school of scientific business management. It is this over-complication that tends to cause so much misunderstanding, leading to poor application. The following description of scrum is intended to capture the spirit of simplicity.

Scrum is a framework for helping people improve the way they do their work. It does this by setting clear expectations and boundaries—two essential aspects that allow self-organization to occur and dysfunction to surface. Scrum uses an iterative process wherein each iteration (aka sprint) is kept as short as sensibly possible, keeping to an even rhythm as it pulses through planning, execution, and reflection. This strict, rhythmical, timeboxing aspect of scrum provides scrum teams with an uncanny ability to unearth organizational dysfunction.

Scrum specifies three roles (scrum master, product owner, and team), requires a prioritized set of requests, a goal for every sprint, and a simple way of measuring progress. Scrum uses timeboxed dialogs to plan, to align on a daily basis, and to inspect/adapt on a sprint basis.

A clear distinction is kept between the "what" (the destination) and the "how" (the pathway). Scrum requires clear focus, commitment and complete transparency at all levels; it embraces, or emphasizes, certain human-centric values including (but not limited to) trust, integrity, courage, and engagement.

Roles

The scrum master is a servant-leader to the team and a change agent within the wider organization. The product owner is the main voice of the customer, establishing a compelling vision and using a process of continuous prioritization to realize that vision. The team is a self-organized, cross-functional, empowered group of individuals who do the work.

Artifacts

A scrum team always maintains a backlog of requests, or goals. The backlog contains all the stuff (we think) we'd like the product or service to do, at any given moment in time. It is a living list, in a continuous state of flux yet always in a prioritized order, which will change over time. Items in the backlog always focus on the "what," and the items with the highest priority must have well-formed outcomes. The sprint commitment is a subset of this backlog, sometimes broken down into work-tasks, which will describe the "how" of realizing the vision of the product. Scrum requires simple metrics, e.g. measures of work remaining, or business value delivered. The metrics should be used to measure truth—not to measure success or failure. Only measures of truth can be trusted not to incite quick-fix behavior in a team.

Dialogs

The team and product owner meet before the start of each sprint to set a sprint goal and plan the work. The team is expected to deliver finished product to meet the agreed goal at the end of the sprint. How the team carries out the work is solely its own concern. Every workday the team members meet around a visual metrics board (e.g. workflow board) to align with one another, and where necessary to request and offer support. At the end of each sprint the completed work is reviewed by stakeholders and consumers who may suggest adaptations. Following the review the team members reflect on their process, seeking ways to improve, and making commitments to change. Every sprint should produce an improved product or service and a more meaningful and engaging process.

This is more or less the description of scrum that has been there since the first scrum book was published in 2001.[1] I have removed it from its software context, dropped some terms in order to keep the focus on the underlying principles and attempted to condense it to its essence. I have neither added nor removed anything.

[1] Ken Schwaber and Mike Beedle, *Agile Software Development with Scrum*, (New Jersey: Prentice Hall, 2001)

Appendix II: How to Hire an Agile Consultant

Now that you have read this book, and hopefully been inspired by some of the ideas herein, you may be wondering how to make this happen in your own organization. There are many ways to get started, including reading more, joining online and local scrum/agile communities, and even just implementing it and learning as you go. You could also engage a scrum consultant or coach to help you get started. Here I offer some guidance for finding the right person for your organization.

Agile is not a prescription. There is no manual. It is not about process, it is about people—it is about respecting people, and guiding them to more effective, more engaged ways of working. Likewise, hiring an agile consultant (a.k.a. coach) should also be person-focused. These days too many clients are being led by big brand names or letting price sensitivity drive their choices. Bad idea. As agile consultancy scales, it dilutes. It's inevitable. The big agencies—the wannabe Accentures of the agile world—may well be able to populate your organization with bodies, perhaps quicker than the small agency or the independent consultant. And they may even be cheaper. But what are you buying? Do you even know?

So, the first piece of advice is: Know who you are hiring. And I mean personally. Engaging a big-name consulting agency could possibly land you with a random consultant, or group of consultants you have never heard of and/or who are unknown in the agile community. Perhaps people with limited experience, primed to follow the company standards—and who knows what those are, or who sets them? With this method of engagement you stand a good chance of getting an inexperienced or compliant consultant.

Here are a few guidelines to finding the right person for your organization. First a couple of things to avoid, followed by a set of things to seek.

1. Don't hire a nameless person.

Don't let a consulting agency promise you "the right person." Chances are the consultant who shows up will have no idea what you need—only what you are asking for, and the two things are rarely the same.

2. Don't let cost and geographical locality be the main criteria for choice.

Start by selecting people who sound as if they know what they are talking about, and have a track record to show it. It doesn't matter if they live further away, or cost more. You will likely get what you pay for, and the value a good consultant can offer is often exponentially better than a low-priced alternative.

3. Go by recommendation.

Ask friends and colleagues in different organizations to make recommendations. If people you know can recommend consultants they have worked with, this can be (but is not guaranteed to be) a good sign. It is at least a better starting point than responding to a Google ad, or a spam email.

4. Plan ahead.

Engage in the agile community through reading blogs, joining discussion groups and attending local agile meetups or gatherings. This way you will get to know who you connect with, who is making sense, who has the experience you think you may need.

5. Research the consultant.

Does the consultant keep a blog? Is he on Twitter? Read the blog posts. Follow the tweets. Why do these things matter? Consultants who themselves engage with the agile community are the risk-takers, the ones not afraid of bad press—just read some of the feedback comments on their blog posts—we call each other out, challenge each other to new ways of thinking. Observe how the consultant responds to criticism. Is he defensive, or embracing?

If the consultant has written a book, read the book—or at least read the reviews on amazon.com, or other booksellers/industry magazines. If there are no reviews, be wary.

Treat resumes only as formal introductions. Resumes are dry, empty documents written to sell the consultant. Don't be sold. Use the principle of attraction over promotion: seek engagement with consultants whose public voices touch or inspire you in some way. Make an effort to find them.

Understand the purpose of LinkedIn. Every consultant is on LinkedIn, and each has carefully vetted feedback comments. LinkedIn is for people who want to do business. Blogs and Twitter are for people who want to engage in community.

6. Seek a consultant who is willing to say "I don't know."

Many consultants will come in with solutions—without knowing what the problem is. This seems to be especially true of agile consultants. Agile in its many guises, e.g. scrum, kanban, is often seen as a cure-all. Process is often imposed—and with the larger, tool-vending companies, a tool is imposed right alongside. Beware of this. Agile tools usually force a process that may be (in fact quite likely is) entirely wrong for your context.

A good consultant will come into your organization with a

beginner's mind. With no solutions. He will come in with innocence rather than expertise. Take this as a good sign. If you have done your homework on the consultant, you have nothing to fear. Solutions emerge from understanding. A good consultant will seek to understand.

7. Meet with the consultant face-to-face before engagement.

Look your prospect in the eyes. Hear how he speaks. Listen for assumptions he may make about your organization. Assess the conversation: is it a pitch, or is it more like a two-way dialog to explore and learn? Again, don't be sold. Listen to your gut.

8. Request an initial assessment—avoid big, up-front commitments.

You are hiring an agile consultant. Be agile about it. Create frequent inspect/adapt moments in the engagement plan to assess value. Ensure a clear exit strategy is implemented at these points, for either party.

In essence, the onus is on you, the customer, to take the time to find the right person. This is not about "staffing" or "resourcing," this is about meaningful engagement with real people, towards the end of effective product creation. Take the time to do this well. In the end your return on investment will be far better.

Index

Contact the author

info@businesscraftsmanship.com
twitter: @tobiasmayer
businesscraftsmanship.com

If you liked this book, please help others discover it by leaving a review on Amazon.com.

More from Dymaxicon

The Elements of Scrum

by Chris Sims & Hillary Louise Johnson

If you are looking for an introduction to scrum that won't leave you feeling like you're trying to puzzle through stereo instructions, check out *The Elements of Scrum*, co-authored by Chris Sims, one of Silicon Valley's foremost experiential scrum trainers, and Hillary Louise Johnson, an award-winning business writer, novelist and editor.

print and kindle editions
available on Amazon.com

44559634R00096

Printed in Poland
by Amazon Fulfillment
Poland Sp. z o.o., Wrocław